HAPPY MUM,
HAPPY BABY

HAPPY MUM, HAPPY BABY

MY ADVENTURES INTO MOTHERHOOD

GIOVANNA FLETCHER

CORONET

First published in Great Britain in 2017 by Coronet
An imprint of Hodder & Stoughton
An Hachette UK company

2

A CIP catalogue record for this title is
available from the British Library

Hardback ISBN: 978 1 473 65120 3
Trade Paperback ISBN: 978 1 473 65121 0
Ebook ISBN: 978 1 473 65125 8

Typeset in Adobe Garamond Pro by Palimpsest Book Production Ltd, Falkirk, Stirlingshire

Printed and bound by CPI Group (UK) Ltd, Croydon, CR0 4YY

Hodder & Stoughton policy is to use papers that are natural,
renewable and recyclable products and made from wood grown in
sustainable forests. The logging and manufacturing processes are expected
to conform to the environmental regulations of the country of origin.

Hodder & Stoughton Ltd
Carmelite House
50 Victoria Embankment
London EC4Y 0DZ

www.hodder.co.uk

For all the mums out there doing their best –
failing and succeeding on a daily basis.
I'm with you!

CONTENTS

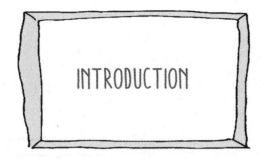

INTRODUCTION

't all just seems a little bit perfect, and we want people to be able to relate . . .' Perfect? I had to chuckle when I once got this note through from an editor about a family piece I'd written. My life is not perfect. I can see how it might look that way from the outside – I have a wonderful 'hands-on' husband, two adorable boys and am somehow managing to keep working – but I'm still winging it like every other mum. I'm still dealing with the same crap of disrupted sleep, sore nipples, and being regularly peed or puked on . . . I'm still struggling with the unbearable reality of mummy-guilt and wondering how it's possible to have a career while still being the best mum I can be to Buzz and Buddy.

I have good days and I have bad days, and even though I try not to dwell on the bad, I sometimes find a good old cry can work wonders at dissipating a low mood or feelings of frustration. Failing that, laughter helps. When things have built up, and are threatening to cause a wobble, they suddenly become less oppressive and easier to handle when you stop and ponder on the ridiculousness of it all. After all, the world is not going to end because your toddler refuses to nap, brush his teeth or put on a pair of shoes, yet those little moments can sometimes feel like huge challenges when they're happening. I occasionally catch myself mid-shoe-wrestle and have a proper giggle at the absurdity of my life. But I wouldn't swap it. Little struggles like that will never outshine the magic of a first smile, an innocent belly-laugh or the first time your child kisses you for no reason other than their own desire to. Moments like that are heavenly!

Right now I'm asking myself why I'm writing this book and wondering if anyone will find a book I've written about being a mum interesting. It's quite a big-headed assumption to make – it's not like writing fiction where you're asking people to invest in the characters you've created. This is more personal. But my own self-doubt aside, I know that certain posts on Facebook, Instagram, Twitter and YouTube (yes, I'm on the lot) really resonate. They spark discussions. Each time I share a blog post or new video where I talk about pregnancy, my changing body or dealing with a toddler and a newborn, I feel an overwhelming sense of togetherness when the comments come flooding in and ladies start sharing their own stories. We've all been through something huge and life-changing, so it makes sense that we want to talk about it with one another.

The bizarre thing I've found about parenting is that every single person on earth seems to have an opinion on how you raise your child and will therefore offer you endless advice. People will passionately tell you the right way to parent, but each person will tell you something entirely different, leaving you with completely conflicting ideas and a frazzled brain.

Because you're instantly hit with this idea of there being a 'right' way to parent, it's easy to feel judged and insecure from day one. And every area is up for debate – whether you fall pregnant instantly or struggle with IVF, opt for a natural birth or a 'sunroof' (C-section), breastfeed or choose to use formula, co-sleep or pop them in their own room straight away . . . There are even judgments cast on the type of child carrier you use! It's bonkers.

Each child is as different as you and I. Therefore, I believe there isn't a one-method-fits-all strategy, no matter how appealing that idea might sound (sorry Gina Ford). I think it's best to gather all the advice given, do your own research and then chuck it all away and give yourself time to figure out a way that works for you and your family. Ultimately we all have the same goal – to bring up a generation of children who are confident, happy and loved – so let's not bash the people doing their hardest to achieve that. Let's empower each other and show support. That's what I've been doing online (mostly. I've also been playing around with Snapchat filters) and I hope to continue that philosophy here while detailing my own take on motherhood. I want to focus on certain aspects of being a mother, share my thoughts on it and open up conversations for other women who might be experiencing something similar.

I'm a real mum and I care about other women. I want us all to feel unified and supported, not isolated and alone, or defensive over the choices we've made in case someone tells us we're wrong.

A health visitor once said to me, 'We do what we have to do to get through it . . .' Buddy was only days old and Buzz was going through a sleep regression. I'd confessed (it even sounds like a sin) that me and Tom were sleeping in different rooms so that Buzz could be in with one of us and not disrupt Buddy. It meant that we could all get some sleep, but it wasn't ideal. I expected her to warn me about creating 'a rod for my own back', but she didn't. Instead she said what I needed to hear. More than that, she meant it. I felt much more confident in the choices we were making after that.

Our words affect others.

We can use them to strengthen or to belittle and crush.

I know what I want mine to do.

1

LET'S START AT THE BEGINNING

LET'S START AT THE BEGINNING

I wondered whether to include this part of my journey into motherhood or not. It isn't a particularly positive, jolly or upbeat section. But it was the start of it all, and it's turned me into the mum I am now. So here goes . . .

always knew that I wanted children. Lots of them. When I envisaged my future I'd see a crowded dinner table on a Sunday, lively with endless conversation and laughter. All my children, their partners and their children catching up as I dished up the crispy spuds and tended to their every need. In my mind they were probably all wearing clothes I'd made for them out of old curtains and ready to burst into song at any minute. I saw my mummy style future as a mash-up of the OXO lady in the adverts and Maria from *The Sound of Music*. Wholesome, caring, doting. Simply perfect. I've always been filled with a need to mother and nurture those around me. Yes, I knew I wanted children. Lots of them.

So imagine my surprise when I came off the contraceptive pill after eight years of being on it and my periods failed to return – and not because I was pregnant. I quite liked it at first – not having to put up with the hassle of Aunt Flo's monthly visits – but the longer she was MIA, the more I started to get concerned. Other little things had started to creep in at this point too – my weight had started to edge slowly upwards, I got random spots on my back and I got hairy (something I always put down to being half Italian and stupidly helping myself to my dad's razor when I was about ten years old to get rid of my innocent blonde upper-lip hairs – idiot!).

Thanks to feeling like I'd become a chubby, spotty and hairy monster I knew something was up, so decided to go to the doctor to find out what. The results of a few tests confirmed that I had PCOS – polycystic ovary syndrome. The doctor handed me a leaflet she'd helpfully printed off the internet telling me all about my ovaries, hormone levels and excess follicles. I looked at it in horror when I noticed one of the subheadings was titled 'fertility'. I asked the doctor about it and her response was not to worry just yet. We could address the issue when it was something I was ready to focus on.

Hmmm . . . I'd got engaged a couple of months before and knew I didn't want to wait too long after my wedding to fall pregnant (in an ideal world), so regardless of her words I was a bit worried. I hadn't realised Aunt Flo's extended vacay could affect my future so dramatically.

Rather than let me dwell on the matter too much in her office, the doctor sent me on my merry way, armed with the 'useful' printout from the internet and a new contraceptive pill to level out my hormones.

The new pill was awful. I'm pretty sure it was made by the devil himself to torture women. I felt sick all the time, had a bloated tummy and felt like I was living in a fog of grogginess. It felt like I was experiencing a few early pregnancy symptoms without any of the joys of actually being pregnant. It sucked.

Eventually a friend of mine who actually *was* pregnant recommended I go to see her baby doctor (we could call him a gynaecologist or obstetrician, but 'baby doctor' seems friendlier). He put my mind at ease straight away. He explained exactly what was going on – basically (this is how I understood it but I'm not a doctor and tend to suffer from selective hearing) my body was producing too much insulin, which in turn made too much testosterone (no wonder I was getting hairy). Testosterone builds the follicles in your ovaries where your eggs are held. Each month one egg matures more than the others and pops out – which is when you're ovulating and babies can be made. As the testosterone was creating too many follicles it meant none of the eggs could mature to a good enough size to hatch and encourage my cycle. But he was confident he could level out my hormones and get me ready to start making bambinos whenever I wanted to. His words were such a relief.

He took me off the monster pill straight away and put me onto a kinder one. He also told me about Metformin, a drug that was originally developed for people suffering from diabetes but can also work wonders for women who don't ovulate.

I felt lighter and happier when I left my new doctor's office, simply because I had a better understanding of what was happening to my body and I felt reassured that there was still a way for me to have children. Plus, there are many women in the public eye who have talked openly about having PCOS and have gone on to have loads of children – like Jools Oliver and Victoria Beckham, to name just a couple.

The appointment made me believe in my body again and gave me a kick up the butt to fill it with goodness and treat it a little better. The new pill was less aggressive on my body and thankfully soon the nasty symptoms from before started to disappear.

After our wedding a year later I came off the pill and started taking Metformin. I was concerned with how having PCOS would affect us making some mini-Fletchers and therefore wanted to prepare my body for what was to come. Although in my mind I always told myself we wouldn't openly admit we were 'trying', more that we were no longer being careful and were tempting fate.

I fell pregnant in the second month of 'not trying'. I couldn't quite believe it so I peed on many a stick to be sure. After a year or two of worrying over whether I could fall pregnant or not, it had happened so easily and incredibly quickly. As I lay on the sofa feeling sick and full of cramps, a huge part of me felt it was too good to be true.

Sadly, it was.

A few days later I woke up to blood. Anyone who's ever experienced that moment knows the paralysing horror that comes with it. I just stared at it for ages, not entirely sure what to do. I turned to Google, obviously, sieving my way through dozens of conversation threads on mummy forums and trying to only read the bits that told me what I wanted to hear (that selective hearing thing again), bending the truth slightly so that I could comfort myself and say it was nothing to worry about as it was only slight spotting. I knew it was more than that.

My boobs were also alerting me to things changing, which I know sounds absolutely ridiculous, but as soon as I found out I was pregnant they'd turned into these full, bouncy mounds – the sort of boobs I'd always dreamed of having. However, that morning they didn't feel the same. They just felt less spongy, as though they'd deflated a little. And then there were those aforementioned cramps. I'd told myself they were just the mild cramps I'd been reading about on the internet and the apps I'd downloaded – they told me to expect a bit of discomfort . . . but how do you know if cramps have gone from mild to something more, or if you're just being a bit of a wimp?

I kept myself busy around the house and tried not to think about it – which in reality meant that I thought about it non-stop.

Annoyingly Tom had to go to a radio show in London that day and then head straight on to Birmingham for a gig. He was gutted to be leaving me, but I told him I was fine, that it was nothing and it would all be OK. I would call if anything changed.

Unfortunately for us, it did.

The red flowed heavier, as though it was mocking me for thinking something so special could be achieved so effortlessly.

I'd only got around to telling two people I was pregnant – even then I knew I should've waited just in case, but I couldn't help sharing our wonderful news. Now I needed to talk. I phoned my friend who knew I was pregnant, sobbing. Since she was the same friend who'd sent me to her baby doctor, she urged me to call him.

They asked me to head into town for a scan.

I can remember the journey into London so vividly – sitting in the back of a taxi on the A40, the sun shining brightly even though it was a cold day in December, and Bob Marley playing on the radio, telling me *Every little thing is gonna be all right . . .*

I'm a sucker for signs.

I thought that it was my one big beacon of hope declaring that a little human was still growing inside me. I actually feel sorry for that gullible version of me trying to hold her crap together, thinking Bob Marley was trying to reassure her from beyond the grave.

My sonographer was waiting for me when I arrived. Unfortunately, the scan showed there was nothing there. No heartbeat. No baby. Nothing. I'd suffered a complete early miscarriage at just over six weeks. The lady delivering the sad news was incredibly sweet and consoling, but every part of me wanted to get out of that room as fast as I could. I wanted to run away. I wanted to go outside and scream at the world. I knew I couldn't hold in the emotions that were bubbling away inside me.

I phoned Tom as soon as I left. He'd just finished his radio interview and they were about to make the drive to Birmingham. The sound of the phone ringing as I waited for him to answer brought him closer to me, but that also meant I was going to have to tell him. And that made it real. I was sobbing before he even answered.

I felt like I'd completely failed him. Us. I might've only known I was pregnant for a few days but I'd been carrying around hopes and dreams of being a mother for two decades. In my first experience of becoming one I'd been unsuccessful. A failure. I would never hold that baby in my arms and the thought was crushing.

After speaking on the phone, Tom drove round to where I was standing sobbing on a London street corner and held me. It was brief but necessary. It wasn't just me who was experiencing the loss.

Tom eventually got back into the car with the boys and told them what had happened while I got into a taxi home. I felt empty, numb and raw, although I experienced an emotional explosion of tears whenever I thought I was getting a grip on the situation. Partly because it was absolutely devastating, but also because I didn't want to accept it.

I felt so utterly alone. The ridiculous thing about not telling anyone that you're pregnant before the twelve-week scan is that no one can be there to comfort you when something like losing a child happens. You're waiting to be told that everything is perfectly fine with your baby, but you need the people close to you to be there if that's not the case.

I longed for the comfort of my family on that day, but I also knew I just wanted to cry and deal with it in my own way. I didn't want the fuss. I didn't want to worry about them being sad about it too. Or for them to be worrying about me.

I sent them a text message.

I know . . . How odd of me. I just couldn't face phoning each of them and telling them. I didn't want to say I'd been pregnant but miscarried. I didn't know how to structure those sentences and put the right words together. But I needed them to know. I needed them to mentally be with me even if I didn't want them physically with me.

My mum phoned me and cried when she heard me crying; having miscarried what would have been my twin when I was only a few weeks in utero, she knew how I was feeling. My dad texted me back to tell me how much he loved me. It was enough knowing they were there. I needed their love.

That night, after she'd heard the news from her fiancé Harry, Izzy Judd (then Johnston) came over to be with me. She didn't try and force a conversation out of me or make a fuss. In fact, the best thing she did was bring around something to do – there was only a week to go until their wedding and she had favours to put together for the guests. We sat for hours putting beautiful little stickers onto packets of seeds and boxes of matches, a job I more than welcomed.

I didn't need someone to talk or who felt the need to try and take the pain away, to pretend it wasn't happening or to give me an endless list of clichés about everything happening for a reason or that it was better now than further on in the pregnancy. It turns out I just needed someone to be there, and I'll be forever grateful to Izzy for her company – and for bringing with her a therapeutic task that stopped me from thinking, even if only for a little while.

I couldn't escape the feeling of loss for long, though; it was back soon enough. I've heard miscarriage referred to as the loneliest grief. It is. It's so insular. So personal. So soul-crushing.

The black cloud of grief followed me for a while.

My periods went back to being irregular and I became angry. Angry at my body for completely failing me and not being good enough. It was a dark time for me, filled with self-loathing. I was eating things I knew wouldn't help my PCOS, I wasn't exercising or taking care of my body. Me and my body had fallen out, big time. I hated it. Every chubby, hairy, spotty inch of it.

Around a month or so later a friend of mine, bless him, gave me a book about the best foods to eat while trying to conceive. It was so incredibly thoughtful of him – he knew how much having a family meant to me and had thought of me when seeing the author being interviewed on TV.

But I wasn't ready.

I had so much contempt for that smart-arse flipping know-it-all book which was going to tell me to cut out everything that was giving me comfort and make me even more miserable. What's more, I hated the fact that I had to stop doing things I loved – like eating spoonfuls of Nutella straight from the jar. How come other people were able to grow babies and I couldn't? Why did their bodies work when mine didn't?

I'd look at other people I saw, or celebrities in magazines, who were pregnant, and feel a heavy sense of foreboding at their capabilities and my failure. Yeah, I wasn't ready to move on. Looking back, I can see that I was still angry, still wounded and still grieving.

Then one day things changed. I forgave myself. I decided I was worthy of love.

I suddenly felt lighter. I picked up the book and started reading, ready to absorb its information. I was ready to do all I could to get my body physically and mentally prepared to grow a human.

I was finally ready to go again.

• • • • •

There is such a huge taboo around the topic of miscarriage. I completely understand that it's not the nicest thing to talk about, nor is it nice to relive the experience while sharing the details with people you know. It is especially hard if friends of yours happen to be trying to get pregnant, or are pregnant already. We don't like to focus on the difficulties that occur when trying for a family – the struggles and the heartache, the inconsolable disappointment and sorrow. We like to think of the ideal – friends announcing they're pregnant and then the delicate cuddles with tiny newborns.

If I think about my own reasons for not previously wanting to know of fertility woes or stories of miscarriage then I'd have to honestly say that hearing of those difficulties made the possibility of them happening to me more real. And that petrified me. I know now how ridiculous that was. It makes me sad to think of how my own insecurities led to me closing my eyes and ears to those suffering in silence.

We're told now that we can't ask women if they want a family – it's even considered rude. But having difficulty conceiving, miscarriage, IVF, or whatever people might be going through when trying to start or expand their families shouldn't be treated like dirty little secrets for people to be ashamed of.

Miscarriage is something that happens. It's totally crap and depressing, but it happens – and as awful and tragic as it is, it's not contagious. I look back and feel mournful over that time and the child I never got to meet, but I realise that if that pregnancy had gone full term then I wouldn't have gone on to have my little Buzz.

Buzz is the biggest silver lining of my life.

2
LEARNING TO START AGAIN

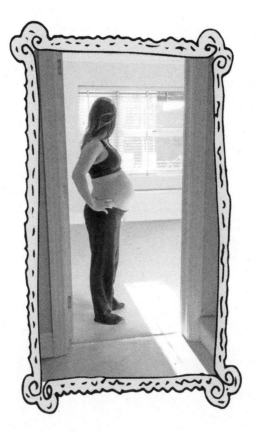

LEARNING TO START AGAIN

To reboot my system, and to help my body do what it needed to do to give my PCOS a kick up the backside, I had a major detox. I cut out caffeine, alcohol, sugar, gluten and dairy. I know what you're thinking: *what was left to eat?* But surprisingly there was lots. For the first time in my life I enjoyed munching on salads and veggies (without feeling like a rabbit) – and didn't feel like I was neglecting myself by choosing not to have chocolate. I actually felt more awake and alive than ever before. I'd also started doing some exercise. I was tempted to write 'more' exercise there, but seeing as I wasn't doing anything physically active in the darker days, that would be a bit of a stretch.

Now I was, I felt amazing.

Aunt Flo was being a bit temperamental, though, and my cycles were really long – usually around thirty-five to forty days. In fact, one month I must've missed a cycle as I went for over eighty-eight days without anything happening. I can't tell you how many tests I took during that time just to make sure I definitely wasn't pregnant. I can still remember the dull ache of sadness that came along with seeing a single line or the words 'not pregnant' appear on those kits. And then the deflating heartache when my period would eventually return, confirming the tests were correct. It was all horrible. I did start to feel the desperation seep in, because as lovely as it was to have her back and see everything was in working order, ol' Flo appearing meant another month of failing to fall pregnant and having those hopes and dreams crushed yet again. Oh, and don't even get me started on the joys of ovulation kits . . . I think I just liked peeing on sticks in the end! Any stick was worth peeing on, just in case it had some good news to share.

In the June of 2013 Tom and I had a big trip planned to surprise his mum and dad in Walt Disney World in Florida. I remember Tom saying I should do a test before we went, just so we knew if I could safely go on rides or not. I can remember telling him I didn't want to do one because I wasn't even on day thirty of my cycle – and I had a thing about testing before day forty. I know it might sound a bit bonkers but I felt like, because of what had happened before, testing earlier was tempting fate somehow, or that if something did go wrong again I could just obliviously shrug it off as a late period and not have to deal with the heartache . . . Anyway, it's something I can't explain very well. I just get fixated on numbers sometimes.

The morning we flew I woke up at 3 a.m. needing a wee. To keep Tom happy, I pushed my worries aside and peed on a stick. I then sat there with my eyes shut, trying to keep myself in a sleepy state so I could just roll into bed and go straight back to sleep when it inevitably declared that I was 'not pregnant' – because there was no way I was. I felt no different to normal – and I'd spent months questioning every little symptom like swollen boobs and nausea so I would've known if something was happening. I was in tune with my body. I knew I wasn't pregnant.

Majorly loud incorrect klaxon alert

Everything stopped when I prised open one eye and saw no 'not' . . . just 'pregnant'. I snatched it up and looked at it a little closer. Yep. That was definitely what it said. I marched into the bedroom, turned on the bedside lamp and shoved it in Tom's sleepy face. Needless to say, he woke up pretty quickly.

· · · · ·

I was incredibly nervous during the first few weeks of that pregnancy because of what had happened previously. I questioned every one of my body's niggles and breathed a sigh of relief every time I wiped to no blood.

When pregnant with Buzz and Buddy I went in for early scans, just to put my mind at ease that everything was OK. Annoyingly, both times I went in too early, meaning the sonographer was unable to find a heartbeat. This led to my lovely doctor warning me about the miscarriage percentages. I think he felt it was his duty to relay the facts and keep me informed about the possibilities. He wasn't doing it to scare me or make me worry. So off we'd trundle with a scan of nothing but a black hole, and a fresh date in our diary for two weeks later. I'd try not to think too much in the time before the next appointment, but it was an inevitable concern.

That worry, that anxiety – all the pain I'd felt previously – it all completely melted away when we heard Buzz's heartbeat for the first time. It was the most comforting and overwhelming sound ever. It was real! It was happening. The love I felt for that oddly shaped little ball of cells that was pumping away with rapid speed was instant. The thought of it makes me want to cry even now.

I didn't want to wait for months for updates on how our little 'Crumb' was doing so we paid for regular scans because I felt I needed the reassurance that everything was OK. I always feel strange when I admit that we opted for private care while pregnant and giving birth. I guess that was the first time I felt vulnerable to other parents' judgment. Although I doubt anyone else even cared, it was probably my own insecurities leaking out. I was just aware that I'd clam up a little when people talked about where they were giving birth or grumbled (and rightly so) at how long it was between scans, because I was aware that I would be having at least eight more scans than them.

I don't like flashy people. I'm not superficial or materialistic and I absolutely abhor it when people talk about money, so I guess I didn't want people thinking of me differently. The truth is I've never gone out a hell of a lot, we don't own a heap of flashy cars or designer clothes – but if there's one thing I wanted to spend money on it was the safe arrival of my unborn child. Why? Because I was flipping scared something was going to go wrong.

It was my trepidation over the pregnancy that led us to leave it as long as possible before telling those outside our family and friendship groups that I was pregnant – something being an author and writing all alone at home made a little bit easier. It wasn't like I was having to sneak off to the staff toilet to puke my guts up, or was found dribbling all over my keyboard after falling asleep mid-email. I could just close myself off and get ready for the hibernation period ahead of me. That being said, when we did eventually share the news in a YouTube video, with the help of a few pumpkins, the love and support we received from well-wishers was so over-whelmingly lovely!

From twenty-three weeks on, I loved my first pregnancy. Firstly, because I'd read that the baby was viable from that point onwards, but also because I was hit by a new appreci-ation for my body. I'd actually go so far as to say that it was the sexiest and most comfortable I've ever felt in my own skin. With my body doing the task it was designed to do, I felt so womanly.

Plus, I felt so cherished – even by people who didn't know me. It was like they'd just see the bump and be donked over the head with a kindness stick. Honestly, the kindness of strangers on the street was unbelievable (things were totally different once the bump turned into a screaming child). I felt like I was a walking miracle and was completely in love with life. It was wonderful.

Unfortunately, my next pregnancy had me feeling slightly different. As my body had only just gone back to 'normal-ish', a little bump popped out straight away – even before I'd taken a test to confirm it. Second time round I felt self-conscious straight away, which wasn't helped by people saying things like, 'Ooh, are you sure you're not having twins?', '*When* are you due?' or simply 'Good God, that's a big bump.' Seriously! I know people mean well, but the things some of them said to me without thinking were enough to make me feel quite sad about my changing body. It was such a contrast to how I'd felt when pregnant with Buzz. More than anything I hated that I'd allowed the words of others to have such power over me.

But more about my body and other people's views on it a little later . . .

3

LABOUR WITHOUT FEAR

LABOUR WITHOUT FEAR

experienced a barrage of advice as soon as I announced I was pregnant – not just from friends and family, but from complete strangers too. I actually had a man ask me if I was going to be breastfeeding my as-yet-unborn child and then start to casually tell me the benefits. I don't think he was being judgmental in manner, nor pervy over my pups, but nonetheless – suddenly my boobs were up for discussion, along with every other part of me.

The biggest conversation-starter, though, was how I was going to get the baby out – foof or sunroof. Eeek, I hadn't given it much thought.

When three separate friends messaged me about the experiences they'd had with hypnobirthing, I knew it was something I wanted to look into a little more – mostly because these women were entirely different in personality, views and lifestyle. One of the women had included a link so eventually I clicked on it and did a bit of investigating. It turned out that this woman, Hollie de Cruz, who funnily enough I'd gone to infant school with (and hadn't seen since we were both nine years old), had loved her experience with hypnobirthing so much that she'd become a practitioner in the field. I mean, that's quite a testament to the method when someone leaves a successful career and makes sharing the joys of hypnobirthing her life . . . right? I emailed her, she sent me a book to read and then she came over to our house twice so that she could pass on all her knowledge and put us into a nice calm state of being.

I'll be honest (I have a feeling I'm going to start many sentences this way while writing this book), I had absolutely no idea what Hollie was going to do with us when she turned up, or indeed what hypnobirthing actually was, so we were a little giddy about the whole affair.

Hollie was amazing. It was amazing. She told us all about the female body, hormones and what happens when giving birth – essentially she dispelled a few myths and explained what a fantastic experience birth could be if we practised using the right tools. I was sold. Especially when she left us feeling ultra serene and tranquil.

I'm still a bit unsure what the official definition of hypno-birthing is and how to describe it – but I'll give it a bash. Hypnobirthing is using breathing and meditation techniques to calm your mind and body, to stop the build-up of adrenaline (the hormone you really don't want while in labour) and encourage the release of the love hormone oxytocin (the hormone crucial to getting baby out). Something Hollie said to me really made sense so I'll pass it on to you now – if we're full of fear and panic during labour, our bodies automatically go into fight or flight mode. That's why adrenaline builds up.

The trouble with that is that it'll pump all the blood and oxygen into your limbs to help you run away from the problem, thus draining those supplies going to your uterus, which is exactly where you need the blood and oxygen to go. With a lack of oxygen going to the tummy muscles trying to help your baby into the world they'll have to work ten times harder and they'll almost judder like a rusty garage door being lifted after years of being kept shut. It'll feel unnatural and probably be uncomfortable. By remaining calm, stilling your mind and focusing on sending your breath around your body and to your baby you're helping build up oxytocin, sending blood and oxygen where it's needed to help ensure the muscles are working in the most efficient way possible.

It gave me a profound respect for the work my body had already done to grow my baby, but also a trust that my body knew, better than I did, what it had to do. After all, the female form is built to birth a child . . . although maybe the old Adam and Eve story with God punishing Eve with the 'pain' of childbirth, probably one of the most repeated stories ever, hasn't done much to separate the word 'pain' from the occasion. On the topic of word association, part of hypnobirthing is getting rid of words that are partnered with negativity, like swapping contraction with surge or wave, pain with pressure, and dilating with opening. I wasn't too fussed about this element of it. Largely because I kept forgetting and felt bad every time I referred to a contraction as a contraction, but also because the words didn't actually bother me at all. I felt calm and didn't feel like the use of these 'negative' words would change that when my birthing experience started.

I practised hypnobirthing techniques religiously – especially in the third trimester. More than anything it was a nice way to step away from my hectic writing schedule and focus on the human growing inside me. Tom was a huge part of the whole thing too, as he used to lead the breathing practice and then read me a little script in the evenings. It was a great thing for us to do as a couple and meant that no matter how busy we were we always found time to come together in the evenings. When talking to friends about the experience Tom always says that the thing he loved so much about hypnobirthing was that it gave him a role in the lead-up to the birth as well as on the day. He was actively involved and ready to do all the faffing so that I could stay focused on the task in hand. I completely understand that the whole thing must be over-whelming for men when seeing their partners experiencing something brand new that takes over their being, but by practising hypnobirthing techniques Tom felt as prepared for the unexpected as I did. Good job!

I appreciate that hypnobirthing isn't for everyone. It felt right for me but I am me and you are you. Don't feel judged over however you decide to bring your child into the world. It's your decision and you have to do what works for you. Likewise, sometimes births don't go to plan and your natural birth ideals can be switched for an emergency C-section. Don't feel guilty if this happens. It's all unpredictable. The only important thing is that your child is born happy and healthy. That's what we're all hoping for. It's all that matters.

4

BIRTHING MY BOYS

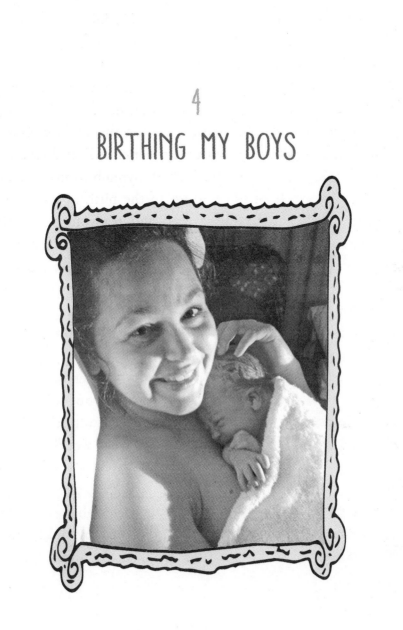

BIRTHING MY BOYS

Everyone always asks about labour stories – it's something we're all fascinated by. So here are mine:

WELCOMING BUZZ INTO THE WORLD

For Danny Jones' birthday on the 12 March 2014 we went with all the McBusted boys, their partners and Danny's family and friends to Tramshed, which is on the opposite side of London to where we live. It was eighteen days before my due date, meaning we were ready for our imminent new arrival and joyful (with a smidge of smugness over being prepared) as we put our hospital suitcase in the boot just in case, even though I was sure I wouldn't need it.

Word of warning: I am rubbish at knowing what is happening to my body. In fact, I must say at this point that I'd had a very slight grumpy tummy since the previous after-noon. But seeing as I'd made a mad dash to the petrol station for some naughty treats and had subsequently stuffed three yum-yums, a whole packet of M&S strawberry cream biscuits and a bag of bacon rasher crisps (I didn't touch the olives I also bought) into my gob while watching *Countdown*, it was hardly surprising. I thought it was my body flipping out over the sugar it had suddenly ingested, seeing as I'd eaten fairly well during the rest of my pregnancy. I didn't even question it. In hindsight I wonder if my sudden desire for these goodies should've been the first sign that labour was on the horizon . . . I was clueless.

Anyway, driving through London on the way to Danny's birthday meal, we passed our chosen hospital where Tom rubbed my tummy and said, 'Now, Crumb, if you're going to come tonight just let us eat our steak first, OK?' Oh, how we laughed at the thought.

An hour later I was sitting talking to Georgia Jones (Danny's now wife) and I just felt this trickling sensation. Nothing major – no Niagara Falls-type gush that I was so used to seeing in the movies, just enough to catch my attention and let me know something was happening. How interesting, I thought to myself. I made my way to the loo and noticed my tights and knickers were wet (I'm grossing out typing that . . . T.M.I.? Ah, we're friends). Now, they weren't dripping, but felt like I'd just got them out of the washing machine, and were a bit slimy. Yes, something was definitely happening. The first person I saw when coming out of the loo was Izzy (there she was again when I needed her). I can remember standing casually washing my hands as I said to her, 'Now I'm not sure, but I think my waters have broken.' The look on Izzy's face was adorable as she asked what we should do. Nothing, was my plan. I'd been told time and time again how long these things take, so I knew there was no point panicking or rushing. My main concern was that I didn't look like I'd wet myself, which thankfully I didn't. Back at the table I sat in my seat next to my wonderful friend Emma Willis and it was as if she knew. She turned to me and asked if I was OK. Trying to stop myself from grinning, I muttered, 'I think my waters have broken.' 'Huh?' came the sound from an excited face across the table. Oh yeah, I guess I should've told my husband first!

We sat and ate steak, and all the while those of the group who knew what was happening kept turning to me with excited grins, looking to see if I was about to pop a baby out right there and then. Harry was on the verge of asking for towels or calling an ambulance. It was hilarious. No one could quite understand how me and Tom were remaining so calm – or why we were still there. But sitting with some of our favourite people in the world just seemed like a fantastic idea to me.

The contractions started coming after I'd gobbled up my main course, so we decided it was time to go. We realised it was the last time we'd be seeing them as just Mr and Mrs – we were about to become a trio. A proper family unit. It was bizarre saying goodbye to them and knowing something so special and life-changing was about to happen. There were lots of hugs exchanged and giggles of excitement as we left.

Back in the car the tightening feelings I was experiencing started getting a little more intense. Not painful exactly, but I was aware things had moved up a gear. Seeing as we were about to drive past the hospital Tom phoned them and they suggested we went in so I could be checked over.

Unbelievably for London, we got a parking spot right outside the front door. As we walked in I remember feeling a little joyous over the fact we'd remembered the suitcase, but also that I'd spent an hour doing my hair and getting ready that night for the meal. I never thought I'd care about how I looked giving birth – I actually don't think it was something I'd given (or give) two hoots about, but in that moment as we walked through the hospital doors I congratulated myself on my glossy mane and how fab it would look in the newborn photos . . . Ha! What a plonker.

'Nothing,' the midwife said, quickly crushing my shiny-hair glee. Even though I was having contractions three minutes apart and a minute in length, I wasn't dilated at all. AT ALL! She even suggested that what I thought had been my waters breaking might've just been me wetting myself. That, or it was just my forewaters and I still had a long way to go. Seeing as she then told me off for my pee being too yellow and not drinking enough liquid, I was inclined to go for the latter suggestion. I didn't smell of wee and wouldn't I know if I had wet myself? Anyway, whether I'd had an embarrassing little accident (I hadn't) or not she sent us on our way, saying she'd probably be seeing us again a few days later.

When we got home at around 1 a.m. the contractions kept coming. I couldn't lie down and sleep (although I made Tom get some shut-eye while he could), so I decided to listen to some Coldplay while doing some of the hypnobirthing breathing I'd learned and bounce on my ball downstairs in the dark. It was very calm, peaceful and atmospheric. I was in a little bubble and it was absolutely lovely. I didn't feel scared or out of my depth. I felt in control and empowered. Even when I had a show (which we had to Google to check what one looked like – it's like a giant bogie) an hour and a half later, I felt fine. I felt ready to just accept whatever was going to happen and trust my body.

I had a bath and continued listening to Coldplay – I can remember actually singing along and swaying about while Tom ran around putting missing items into the suitcase (laptops and chargers) along with anything else he randomly thought we might need . . . It makes me chuckle to think what Tom put in during that time. Panic-packing in the calmest way possible.

Anyway, around 4.30 a.m. Tom phoned the hospital again and told them about the show. They said that I could go in 'if I wanted' but that it would take a while so I was better off staying at home as long as I could. We weren't too fussed as I was really happy and relaxed at home. While waiting to see how things would progress, we sat downstairs, had some cereal and pottered around for a bit. At 8.30 a.m. my baby doctor called to see what was going on as he'd heard about our late-night hospital visit. He was off to France that night, so encouraged me to drive into town so he could take a look at what was going on.

I don't remember much of that journey – apart from listening to a mixture of hypnobirthing tracks and Tim Minchin (part of hypnobirthing is about listening to and watching things that make you happy – Tim cracks me up). I thought we were only in the car for half an hour, but according to Tom it actually took an hour and a half thanks to it being rush hour, with us getting to my doctor at around 10.30 a.m.

I was scanned right away and my doctor voiced his concern over the lack of fluid surrounding the baby, so asked to examine me. After having a quick look he glanced up at me with a puzzled expression on his face.

'Gi, have you not been having any contractions?' he asked in his thick Scottish accent.

'Yeah . . . I'm having one now,' I replied, my voice as calm as anything.

'Mmmm . . .' He nodded. 'Tom, come and have a look at this.'

I watched as Tom shuffled down 'the business end'.

'That's your baby. You're already six centimetres.'

I blooming knew something was happening!

Now, I don't mean it to sound like the whole of my labour with Buzz was based around food, but before taking that short walk from my doctor's clinic to the labour ward at the hospital we decided to go for brunch. It was something we did after every baby scan, so it felt like a good idea. Plus, we'd been talking about it in the car on the way in and I quite fancied it. Yes, that makes three meals while knowing I was in labour. Friends of mine won't be surprised by that . . . I like my food.

We got to the hospital at around midday. Time seemed to fly by very quickly again. We watched Michael McIntyre, listened to more Coldplay, splashed around in the birthing pool and Tom gave me a few back massages and ate loads of jelly babies (Tom did, not me). Hypnobirthing was working. Having said that, there was a moment later in the afternoon where there seemed to be a switch, where everything really intensified. I was obviously going through the transition stage and it was a little more effort to keep calm and on top of my breathing. This is where Tom was a huge support, reminding me to breathe every time my face creased into a frown – simple but incredibly important. I can't tell you how powerful those breaths were: breathing into wherever I felt uncomfortable and feeling that discomfort dissipate showed me just how incredible the technique was.

Once I was in the final stage of labour I can honestly say it felt like I'd taken every drug known to mankind, even though I'd done nothing but breathe. I can even remember cracking jokes and making Tom, the midwife Gina (I absolutely adored her and in my spaced-out state thought she was some kind of guardian angel) and my baby doctor laugh . . . I found myself VERY funny.

Buzz Michelangelo Fletcher entered the world at 7 p.m. on Thursday, 13 March 2014, weighing 6lbs 3oz. Holding him in my arms and feeling the warmth of his skin against mine was the most magical and surreal moment of my life. I just couldn't believe that I'd made him. I'd carried him for nine whole months, and there he was – squawking in my arms.

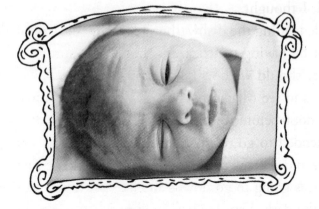

With regard to giving birth, I wouldn't say I laughed or breathed Buzz out, but straight away afterwards I was referring to the whole birthing experience as 'the most amazing thing I've ever done'. It was incredible.

Now, back to food . . . someone once told me that the tea and toast you eat straight after giving birth (terribly British and quite a standard offering) is the best you'll ever have. I blooming agree.

WELCOMING BUDDY INTO THE WORLD

Seeing as Buzz had arrived so early I was a bit miffed when baby number two didn't decide to arrive at exactly the same point in my pregnancy. I know it was a little silly of me to even think he would, but minds are a bit silly sometimes and, like I said earlier, I have a thing about numbers.

At thirty-eight weeks and four days we were watching the BAFTAs (which we'd recorded from the previous night) when I felt a cramping, period-type pain. I remember taking a look at the clock but not thinking much of it. It came again twenty minutes later, then ten, then five.

Odd, I thought.

While loading the dishwasher I casually told Tom I thought I might be having contractions, but wasn't sure.

'What should we do?' he asked.

'Wait and see what happens next,' I replied, closing the dishwasher door before we headed upstairs to get ready for bed. I had intended to go to sleep, but the contractions were getting stronger and I knew there was no way I could lie down. I told Tom I was going to go downstairs like last time and sit on my ball in the dark. Very quickly I jumped to having minute-long contractions, three minutes apart – and they were intense to the point where I found sitting down uncomfortable. Every now and then I'd jump up as my body had this bizarre tightening feeling that I didn't recall having when in labour with Buzz. I kept doing all of my hypnobirthing breathing, which for the most part helped me feel like I was in control and nice and calm. At around 11.20 p.m. I thought I'd watch a bit of Micky Flanagan to lighten the mood, but I only got a couple of minutes in before I decided it was time for Tom to call the hospital. Even though my waters hadn't broken (I think part of me was waiting for that) and I hadn't had a show, I just knew that things were happening far quicker than they had before. Plus, we had to factor in getting Buzz over to Tom's parents' house and driving half an hour into London. The midwives agreed that it would be a good idea to start making our way there.

We faffed a bit as we made sure we had everything (more calm panic-packing), and then Buzz had a total meltdown at being woken up and put into the car – rightly so. I'd be highly confused and pissed off too if someone snatched me from my nice warm bed while it was dark and cold outside. The poor little thing. We had tried to prepare him in the lead-up and continued explaining it all to him in the car, but it was a bit much for him to take in. When we got to his nanna's it seems he thought it was just the start of another day, as he asked to play 'sticks and drums' as usual. He obviously wasn't allowed to, but apparently it took two hours for him to concede defeat and go back to bed and to sleep. What an adventure!

Once Buzz was dropped off we set off for the final leg of the drive into town. I breathed, and breathed, and breathed. I was also glued to my contraction timer. I didn't have one with Buzz but in this instance I felt oddly comforted that I could see exactly when the contractions were about to come. Once again I zoned out and focused on my body, although I was aware that I was catching my breath every now and then at the intensity and speed of it all.

When we arrived I didn't want to be dropped off at the hospital door, I wanted to stick with Tom (I didn't want to be stranded on my own or for him to have to leave me up there), so we parked and then took twenty minutes to walk the usual two-minute walk because I kept having to stop and let my body do its thing.

At this point I was a little concerned. I couldn't remember feeling this way with Buzz, and I know I shouldn't have been comparing the two births, but this was so intense. It was as though I could literally feel my cervix dilating. Because it was all so powerful I wasn't sure if I'd be mentally and physically able to have the same magical birthing experience as before – it felt too much. Basically I was whacked with a big old dose of self-doubt. Probably because I thought Buzz's birth had been so amazing, and this didn't feel like that. It felt like my body had a mind of its own and it was taking control.

We walked into the hospital at 1.17 a.m.

First of all the midwife wanted to monitor me and the baby for twenty minutes, just so they could see what was happening. I can't tell you how uncomfortable I was having those belts around my tummy and having to lie back on the bed. I felt like The Incredible Hulk and wanted to just get up and rip them all off while turning neon green. Plus, the contractions had ramped up another gear, with the head midwife coming in and commenting that they really were 'on top of each other'.

Yes. Yes, they flipping are, I thought.

Tom kept me calm by putting on an episode of *New Girl* (it was our obsession at the time) and giving me something to eat – a protein bar, which was blooming disgusting, so I quickly moved on to the Choco-bons that were meant to be saved for afterwards . . . oops!

After twenty minutes of what felt like torture (aside from the entertainment and delicious snackage) the belts were taken off and I was examined. I was five to six centimetres. Not amazing – let's face it, we'd all love to go in and be told the path is clear – but 'five to six' was better than nothing. Plus, I'd been uncomfortable on my back so knew I needed to get myself feeling relaxed again.

The birthing pool was ready, so I quickly nipped to the loo before getting in. While perched on the bog I had this extremely weird sensation come over my body. It was as though it was seizing all my power, and it caused my tummy muscles to tense in a bizarre wave and then a squeezing motion.

Then it suddenly stopped and there was nothing.

Odd.

I got into the birthing pool while telling Tom what had

happened, was quickly enveloped in the gorgeously hot water and got back to watching *New Girl*.

Ten minutes later the feeling came again.

'My body is doing something,' I said to the midwife.

'Don't fight it, just let it do its thing,' she replied.

Well, I had no flipping choice. There was zero per cent chance of me battling the force with which my body convulsed, tensed, squeezed, pulsed and then relaxed as though nothing had even happened. I experienced this five times, they lasted about thirty seconds each and were a minute or two apart (I think). Here's a brief insight into what happened with each one.

One: My waters broke.

Two: I felt as though I could feel the whole baby move downwards through the birth canal, ready to make its escape.

Three: I could feel the top of the head.

Four: The head was out.

Five: At 2:26 a.m. Buddy Bob Fletcher arrived into the world and I scooped him into my arms straight away, completely astounded by what had just happened.

I couldn't stop laughing. In my mind I'd only just got into the pool – I mean, we hadn't even finished a whole episode of *New Girl* . . . what happened to me being just five or six centimetres dilated? My body had taken control, decided he was fully cooked and expelled him from my body with such force that Buddy ended up having bloodshot eyes for weeks (we joked that he looked like a villain in a superhero movie), and I had lost all feeling in my index finger. Yeah, not the usual injury you'd associate with giving birth, but I think I'd held on to the side of the pool so tightly that I managed to damage a ligament in the process. It took months for the feeling to return completely.

Back to the delivery room, and my love for Buddy was as intense as the birth. I've read a lot about fearing the inability to love subsequent children as much as you do your firstborn, but it wasn't something I'd been particularly concerned about. I didn't feel the new-mum fear I'd felt with Buzz, or shocked that there was suddenly a baby in my arms. I just felt deliriously in love. So much so that I made Tom grab his camera and take photos of us together, naked in the dirty pool water. I didn't care. It was such a magical moment. That feeling continued as we got to our room at 4.30 a.m. and just stared at the newest family member while munching on burger and chips.

But there was an overwhelming sense of something missing. Buzz. We couldn't wait to go home and introduce little Buddy to his big brother, so even though we'd booked to stay for two nights, we barely stayed fifteen hours. By 4 p.m. on the day he was born, we were back on the A40, taking him to his new home. We just wanted to be united as a foursome and had an overwhelming sense that Buzz should be included in this new adventure from the start. Part of me felt guilty that he might have thought his new little brother had taken his mummy and daddy away. I didn't want him feeling pushed out or jealous. In our eyes he was as much a part of what was happening as we were. We were bringing him home a playmate. I wanted him to be excited by that and not fearful or upset.

When we got home Buzz was running around being a little nutter, knowing that something exciting was happening because his nonno (my dad) and his nanna and Ewad (Tom's parents) were all there. It took him about fifteen minutes to even register Buddy, but when he did – when he walked over and gave him a kiss and wanted to cuddle him and shower him with affection – my love for him grew to levels I'd never even known existed. It was as though a whole new rush of love and emotion had been unleashed. It was so special to see my two boys together and I'm in awe on a daily basis of the bond they share. They adore each other.

5
REALITY BITES

REALITY BITES

vividly remember being in the hospital with our fresh little newborn Buzz (complete with crusty blood on his head because we were told not to wash him even though all the creamy goodness had been rubbed off) and just watching him non-stop. Every little thing about him was absolutely fascinating. The way his chest would rise and fall with each breath (occasionally erratically which totally freaked me out), the way his tiny feet were really angled up into his shins from where he'd been positioned in the womb, and the way his lips would fall into the perfect little pout when he slept. He was adorable and perfect.

It felt so surreal for Buzz to actually be there in front of me – something that was probably heightened by the fact he was almost three weeks early. I couldn't believe I'd literally become a mum overnight. I felt a little clueless, so was really grateful to the staff at the hospital for giving us some guidance on what we were actually meant to be doing with him. Mind you, he didn't really do much. We were all faffing and fussing around him, but he just slept. I actually asked the midwife at one point when he was going to start doing 'stuff', like simply be awake. But it turns out that is the way of newborns – they sleep, poop, feed, then sleep some more. How blissful!

After two nights in the hospital we decided it was time to go home and properly start our life as parents, aka responsible humans who didn't just rely on midwives for guidance on just about everything. While Tom went to fetch the car I got Buzz dressed in his first proper outfit – a little pair of comfy white trousers with star-patterned knee patches, a white bodysuit, white hat and creamy grey cardigan. It was a collection of gender-neutral clothing from Mothercare, which turned out to be far too big for him thanks to his early arrival. The trousers were so baggy around the waist he could've fitted in there twice, and the sleeves of the cardi had to be rolled up several times (cue the start of my obsession with buying kids' clothing online!).

He looked so dinky when I strapped him into the car seat it made me want to cry. Perhaps it was because of the undeniable innocence he represented, and the fact he had so much to discover, or maybe it was because I'd just given birth and was majorly exhausted with hormones flying everywhere. Either way, we'd been in a bubble of new familyhood without any external pressures or realities for a couple of days; it was time to let our previous life collide with our new one.

When we eventually left the hospital room a wave of nerves suddenly crept up on me. I had to resist the urge to constantly check with the midwives we were actually allowed to leave them. I couldn't believe we were being trusted with this precious cargo and let free into the big bad world.

In my head I was like a prison inmate seeing real daylight for the first time in a decade, walking through the exit doors and finally being labelled a 'free man', or in my case, a new mum . . . It felt refreshing and uplifting to be back with society, but at the same time oppressive and terrifying.

I wasn't the same human I'd been when I walked through those same glass doors forty-eight hours earlier. My life had been altered and I'd changed as a result – as had my outlook on the alien and stark world outside the hospital. It seemed harsher, more threatening and loud, causing me to feel highly protective towards our baby.

When we eventually got home (I sat in the back with Buzz for the hour-long journey – blooming traffic) we laid Buzz in his Moses basket in the living room, made ourselves some tea and just sat and stared at him some more. He was utterly perfect.

• • • • •

The first few weeks of having Buzz home were mayhem and I felt completely out of my depth in my new role as a mother.

Now, how's that for a statement?

Yes, it seems Buzz had lured us into a false sense of security at the hospital, and shit was about to get real. Really real.

Breastfeeding wasn't coming naturally (but I think that deserves its own chapter) and I was getting hardly any sleep. Something my former ten-hours'-sleep-a-night-I-can-sleep-anywhere-anytime smug self found pretty difficult to come to terms with. It wasn't just the lack of sleep, but being startled awake without warning that left me feeling like I'd found myself in the twisted torture camp of Satan . . . OK, slightly dramatic, but being graced with only an hour's sleep every two hours was pretty detrimental to the happy vibes I thought I was going to be whacked with as soon as I became a mum. Where'd all the oxytocin gone? I needed that bastard love hormone to come back!

And then there was the crying. All the crying . . . Pretty much all of the books I'd read while studying how to be the perfect mum told me I'd learn to understand my baby's needs by his cry. Er, no. Not at all. I couldn't tell whether he was hungry, wet, tired, bored or simply wanted a cuddle – the only one I was good at was seeing whether he had wind, and that's only because a midwife had told me about the blue patch they get above the lip if they have it. Although I wouldn't have realised wind was the cause just from listening to the wails coming from his mouth. To be honest I don't think I ever really listened to the crazed high-pitched screeching that sounded more like a piglet being taken to slaughter than a tiny little baby. I was so caught up in getting it all right that I closed my ears to the noise and just told myself I couldn't understand it while calmly getting into a flap.

Yes, a calm flap. I was a total duck – calm on the surface but flapping like crazy underneath as I frantically fought to sort out the situation. I wanted to seem like I was in control, but in reality whenever those cries kicked in I'd feel the fear levels rising and the blood in my body get a little hotter – something that never failed to bring on the 'mum sweats'. I hated the thought that people would look at me and realise that I didn't know what the flip I was doing. I wanted to be the mum who had her shit together and took the whole thing in her stride.

I didn't.

I really didn't.

There were times in those early days where a cry from Buzz eventually led to me crying too. Tears of frustration. Tears of failure. Tears of sadness that I wasn't the wonderful mum I thought I was going to be. Just tears because crying with him felt like the only option I had left. I cried so much. Not usually in front of friends or people who came to visit (though some-times it couldn't be helped), but rather when he was eventually asleep and I'd managed to achieve a moment of peace. When I felt I'd finally managed to be a fraction of the mum he deserved.

One glorious occasion of being overwhelmed led to Tom finding me standing naked in the middle of our bedroom, post-partum body wobbling everywhere, milk dripping all over the floor from my engorged boobs and me sobbing my heart out while Buzz slept peacefully in his SnuzPod. I'd been trying to feed him, burp him and then get him back to sleep for hours. I was in pain and emotionally drained.

I was broken.

I broke quite a few times.

I'd put so much energy into and emphasis on getting the labour perfect, and was thrilled that I'd managed to achieve the experience I'd longed for – you could say it was a textbook hypnobirthing experience – so I was a bit miffed that my baby wasn't textbook, or that I wasn't a textbook mum.

I felt so unprepared and so utterly crap in my new role of having someone depend on me for absolutely everything. Not because I didn't want him to depend on me, but because there were moments I felt hopelessly helpless. Moments where Buzz would be screaming in my face, *his* face going flaming red, his eyes looking like they were going to bulge out from their sockets, and I'd feel completely incompetent for not knowing how to stop him. I hated when other people handed him back when he started crying, invariably saying, 'Oh, he wants his mummy.' No, I used to think. No, he doesn't. He doesn't know who I am. He doesn't love me yet. You're handing my baby back but he's not going to stop crying. You're going to see how terrible I am. You're going to see I'm a bad mum.

I wondered about my capability. I doubted my natural instincts to mother. I thought I'd made a huge mistake and that the whole parenting malarkey just wasn't for me, which is hardly the best thought to be having when you're shushing your baby at 3 a.m. while trying to get him to latch on to your incredibly sore boobs. In those moments I felt numb to life. It's quite upsetting to look back now and remember how disconnected I felt, actually.

I was faced with emotions that I knew deep down I didn't really feel but in those moments of panic and tiredness they seemed very real. I felt overwhelmed with the simplest of tasks and would crumble easily – especially in the dark of night.

I'd worry that my patience wasn't great enough, and that's something I hate admitting but am glad I was aware of. I'd feel the fragility of the little baby boy in my arms and know how easy it would be for me to do something stupid in frustration and despair. The horrifying thought would be enough to sober me into calmness, reminding me that I was the adult. That he was just a little newborn learning to express his emotions, wants and desires, completely new to this alien world.

Because of all those feelings, though, I worried about the bond being created. I mean, I knew I was hit with an overwhelming feeling of love when he was first born and adored him beyond comprehension – just thinking about it now causes a swell of love to run through me – but I was worried I didn't love him enough, that our connection wasn't working, or that the bond wasn't right. I was focusing so much on what I should be doing, thinking or feeling that I wasn't allowing myself to stop and just embrace it and enjoy time with the child I'd longed for. It was so confusing because I was aware of the monumental love surging within me, but something was stopping me from really feeling it.

I can even remember telling my dad that I didn't think Buzz liked me very much. 'Don't say things like that. You're his mum. Of course he does. You're the most important person in the world to him,' was what he replied. Those words have stuck with me ever since. Just something about having my wise dad say them to me made them a little truer. Not only did I not say that sentence ever again, but I've not felt that way since. I know there will be times in life when we feel disconnected, when Buzz slips away and becomes independent, but I will always be his mum – and that means something. I look at the relationship my dad has with his mum, my nonna, and I'm always touched by the respect and fondness between them. My nonna is actually an idol of mine – she's such a force to be reckoned with, such an incredibly strong woman with a huge booming voice and a cackle of a laugh, but there is a tenderness towards her children that's so endearing, as are the huge levels of respect they have for her. She is still the boss! Even though she's ninety-five years old and her children – my dad, aunt and uncles – are in their sixties and over, they're still her babies. I know my babies will grow and become adults with their own minds and life goals, and that there will be times when we don't necessarily see eye to eye, but it's my job to raise them into brilliant humans, to shower them with love and encourage them to pursue their dreams. If all I have to give is love, then my children will be very rich indeed . . .

I'm digressing!

Thankfully everything was far simpler with Buddy, but maybe that's because he was the second baby and I was able to take it in my stride a little more. Life was generally a lot calmer, even though Buzz had become an all-singing, all-drumming toddler who liked to make a lot of noise – all of the time! Not that Buddy ever seemed fussed by the chaos. By the time he arrived I felt far more confident in my mummy role, yet those mum sweats weren't (and still aren't) ever too far away.

Funnily enough, a couple of days before this book was announced I was out for lunch with my mate Emma Willis and our children. After a wonderfully peaceful morning Buzz and Buddy decided they no longer wanted to play by my rules. Buzz didn't want to sit in his chair and kept trying to run away, and Buddy wouldn't stop crying. Cue me standing up for the entire meal, jiggling Buddy on my hip and pathetically urging Buzz (it was before we introduced the 'thinking' step) to stay in his seat. It was a disaster, so the thought of this book being announced and people thinking I was going to be giving them tips on how to raise the perfect human caused me to have quite a chuckle (and to panic!). If you're still hoping that's what this book is then you should stop reading now! Like I've said all along – this isn't a tip book, just a very honest account of my experience of motherhood so far. Be warned: I have a tendency to overshare . . . but I think you'll have realised that already!

6

HEAL AND RECOVER

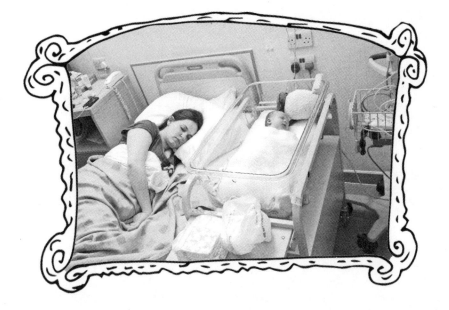

HEAL AND RECOVER

Now, I bosh it when it comes to giving birth. I'm flipping ace at it and I love it – but I'm crap at the recovery part. I'm pants at sitting down and doing nothing while my body heals . . . and both times my body needed healing. Yes, first time round my lovely doctor gave me a dreaded episiotomy. It was something I really didn't want, but in the moment I just wanted to do whatever I was told was best for my baby. Second time round, I tore. Surprisingly the tear was much easier to recover from, but maybe that's because I knew more about not doing too much and what could happen if I did.

So, back to first time round . . .

I'd just given birth to Buzz and felt like a superhuman. Seriously, I knew I didn't need to stay in bed – my body was amazing and could do anything I wanted it to. It had just spent nine months growing a human and then birthed it. Of course it could handle walking up and down the stairs dozens of times a day, doing loads of washing and making hundreds (slight exaggeration) of cups of tea and coffee when our lovely visitors came to cuddle our wrinkly newborn.

My body was amazing and could do ANYTHING.

That was my first epic fail as a mother – trying to be Wondermum and do it all when I should've sat back and let others look after me. I just wanted it to look like I was on top of everything. I wanted people to turn to each other when they left and say, 'Oh, isn't she doing great – she's so calm and in control.'

I was a stubborn mule.

Even when people did offer to make the drinks for me, or asked if I wanted them to unload the dishwasher or put a load of washing on, I refused and shrugged off the idea. It wasn't that I didn't need help (I'd try to frantically clean/throw things in cupboards before people arrived), it was more that I was too proud to accept that them doing just one little job like cleaning up the kitchen would be like winning the lottery. I simply wanted to be able to do everything. I didn't want to admit that the endless stream of guests coming over to cuddle our newborn was just too overwhelming. I managed to keep my crap together while people were over, but then would inevitably fall apart during the evenings and in the dead of night. I even cried at one point because my aunt told me I couldn't eat sun-dried tomatoes when breastfeeding because it was bad for the baby, right after I'd just shoved half a dozen in my gob (turns out you are allowed, but it's hard to keep up when the 'rules' are constantly changing).

But, oh, the pain!

Now, I didn't use the word pain with either of my labours . . . but bloody hell, recovery when you've got stitches hurts. I felt like the biggest wimp ever moaning when I hadn't heard any other woman speak of the aftermath before (it's always the birth people talk of, never do they share the woes of the time afterwards when you've got a bruised and swollen foof), and so I ploughed through. I told myself what I was experiencing was normal and that I was just being a bit pathetic. I walked up and down the stairs several times a day, waddled back and forth from the kitchen with fresh cups of tea, and generally moved around as though my nether regions weren't being held together by a thread. What an error.

I was so sore. Every now and then there'd be a sharp tug that would make my eyes water and me whimper, literally stopping me in my tracks. When the visiting midwife asked if I wanted her to have a look and check it over I practically jumped at the offer. She said it was fine, but that I needed to slow things down a little. To sleep when the baby slept and everything else you know you should be doing when you're a new mum. Basically, taking care of yourself. I must say, the best bit of advice she gave me was to bring everything I needed for the day down with me in the morning, cutting the number of times I travelled up and down the stairs by about ninety-nine per cent. I had been stupidly going back into Buzz's nursery every time he'd done a pee – which with newborns is so often it's a joke. Thanks to her I decided to have a fully loaded changing bag and nappy changing area set up downstairs too. The only thing I went upstairs for after that was when I needed to use the loo myself. Call me a prude, but I just wanted to have the privacy of my own toilet when it came to sanitary pads, leakages and horrible smells – it was all going on.

Actually, while we're on the subject of being on the loo, I must tell you what happened to me a few days after giving birth, simply because I had NO IDEA such a thing happened.

I was in the middle of peeing when I suddenly felt like I was doing a number two . . . only I wasn't. The muscles down below started to feel like they had in the delivery room. I was pushing something out (which was even more terrifying because of the stitches), but it certainly wasn't a poop. Wrong hole! Being the crazy woman that I am I decided to catch it before it made it into the water below and was greeted with the horrific sight of a huge clot of blood, almost the size of my palm. I gave a panicked shout to Tom: 'Erm, honey . . .' I wasn't quite sure how to verbalise the fact that I'd birthed something else. We stared at it in morbid fascination for a few minutes before phoning my doctor – something I'm so glad I did before hitting Google. After describing it all in great detail I was told it was nothing to worry about, just my body's way of having a good old clear-out up there and getting rid of the unwanted debris. Since then, though, I have been on forums and seen people discussing it, and a bloody lump is not always something to be blasé about. It's definitely worth calling a professional about if it happens to you, as it all depends how long after the birth it happens and also the size of it. Now what was it I was saying about how I might over-share in this book?

The uncomfortable pains kept coming. I treated myself to a few hot baths with milk and tea-tree oil (someone said it would help, but it hurt like a b*@%h), but that just made it worse. When the midwife came again I said I was fine, though, and not to worry about checking – simply because it had been fine before. Plus, it's blooming embarrassing to have someone looking down there at your war wound, especially if it *was* all fine and I was just being a moaner.

Saying that, I eventually let Tom have a look (bless him).

I think he was more surprised at the bruising but he was very sweet with me and said he didn't notice anything odd. Now, I know he's my husband and was partly responsible for what had happened down there (it takes two people to make babies – quick science lesson for you there), but *he* convinced *me* to let him look. I must say, it wasn't the sexiest moment of my life – however, we've made another baby since, so it's clearly not scarred either of us. Ha!

You're probably wondering why I didn't look myself with a mirror. Well, I never even thought of it! Baby brain led me to completely forget how those handy little reflective gadgets work. Once my brain started working again and I remembered their existence, I did use them later when 'assessing the damage' (and then became obsessed with checking after having Buddy).

• • • • •

Eight days after I gave birth to Buzz his middle finger became inflamed, with yellow pus in the nail groove, and his eyes became all gloopy. It was the strangest thing – one minute he was fine and then the next time I fed him he couldn't open one of his eyes and his finger looked incredibly sore. I got an emergency appointment with the GP. He had an infection called paronychia in his finger (caused by bacteria getting under the skin – it's very common with newborns) and conjunctivitis in his eyes. He needed antibiotics, but the doctor felt he should go to A&E, as newborns can't just be administered medication willy-nilly. It all sounded perfectly understandable and straightforward. We sat waiting in paediatric A&E for over five hours. It was pretty miserable to be honest, but things turned traumatic when the next appointed doctor tried and failed to put a cannula in the back of Buzz's tiny little hand. Seriously, we thought we'd already heard Buzz's cry, but that shrill scream of pain is one I'll never forget. Tom's parents had joined us (we were there for so long they thought we might want company) and we all wept at the sound of our precious newborn's cries of agony. Gah . . . it makes my heart ache just thinking about it.

When the cannula was finally in and drugs given (the whole debacle took a further two hours) we were sent home WITH THE CANNULA STILL IN, a handful of antibiotics to administer at home and instructions to head back for 7 a.m. the following day so he could receive more medication via the IV drip. We were in a whirlwind of confusion and just happy to be leaving A&E. It was only when we got in the car that we decided we really weren't comfortable with what had happened. Our baby still had a needle coming out of his hand, albeit wrapped in a bandage, but we didn't know what to do with it and it seemed like a huge quantity of medication for one so small. It all just felt a little wrong. So we phoned the private hospital he was born in. They said it sounded fine but were uncomfortable knowing he'd been given the drugs and then sent home. Apparently newborns should be monitored afterwards, simply to make sure they aren't allergic to anything they've been given. They suggested we went back in to see them and have Buzz looked at on the children's ward. We happily agreed. Well, I say happily, but I definitely cried lots while packing up our things (and simultaneously feeding Buzz – multi-tasking never looked sexier). I realise we were lucky he only had two minor infections when compared to other illnesses newborns can pick up or be born with, but that cry was horrible! I felt like I'd failed him as a mother and that it was my fault he was in pain.

Talking of pain, I was still in lots of it myself. Once we'd pulled up outside the hospital I can remember saying to Tom that I might ask one of the midwives to pop down the following morning and check me over.

It turned out I couldn't wait that long.

When Buzz was happily settled after being checked over, my attention swung back to me and my foof – simply because it was so bloody angry at me. I couldn't sit, stand, lie – everything was torture. Perhaps the hours sitting on a chair in A&E had put too much pressure on my tender bits. All I knew is I was in agony. A midwife and doctor came down from the maternity ward to assess the situation. It turns out one of the inner stitches had come loose and I'd caught an infection as a result. I know getting an infection isn't a good thing, but I have to tell you that I was incredibly relieved. Relieved to know I wasn't just being pathetic and that I was surrounded by people who could take care of the situation . . . and give me drugs! Having never given birth before or experienced healing from any sort of stitches, let alone ones down there, I hadn't known what I should or shouldn't be feeling. Part of me thought it was normal to be in that much pain, and unfortunately, a large part of me just didn't want to admit that it was too much for me to bear. I mean – I'd just breathed a baby out of my body without even a puff of gas and air. I didn't want to admit my body was anything but wonderful. I now realise my body still was, and is, blooming marvellous, but after going through such a huge event as giving birth it just needed a lot more TLC. I realised much later, after having Buddy, when I was told to keep everything down there 'as dry as possible', that the blooming hot baths I'd been recommended would have done me no favours and had probably caused the stitch to soften. Well, you live and learn.

Buzz and I stayed in hospital for five days while getting over our infections.

Surprisingly, five days in bed not worrying about anything other than my baby and myself was bliss. We still had visitors and welcomed them, like my sister Giorgina and her husband Chickpea Lee (a silly nickname given to him by my family on a drunken night out), who came a couple of times with takeaway pizzas for dinner, but the visitors were far fewer.

While we were there, everything seemed far more manageable without the external pressures of everyday life. I could rest, sleep when Buzz slept, and just pour love into him. It took me stopping for our bond to really start growing. Although I think seeing him on that hospital bed writhing in pain awoke a fierce desire to protect him too.

While I was recovering there was one thing I longed to do when we got home, and that was go for a walk. I wanted to be like all the other mums and dads we'd seen pushing their newborns around our local lido or aquadrome. At that point in time just walking around the house seemed like an achievement, so walking a mile or two seemed like a distant dream. It took me a month to actually venture out, but soon I was going for short walks around the block. In fact, as we live on a hill I'd drive to a flatter part of town and walk around there instead. That then built up to me being able to walk more frequently and for longer periods of time and before long I was licking a 99 Flake while strolling around the lido, enjoying the spring sunshine. Dream achieved.

While I was going through it, the healing process felt like it was taking forever, but actually, in the grand scheme of things, it took no time at all. I'll talk more about the wonder that is the female body later on (surprise surprise), but for now I just want to say how thrilled I was to find the discomfort slipping away and feel normal again – or just not register anything uncomfortable, which I guess is the same thing.

Our bodies are remarkable when given the time to heal, something I've seen again recently with my sister after she had an emergency C-section to deliver my niece Summer Rae, who was breech with her head stuck up in Giorgie's ribcage. Giorgie and her new family were staying with us at the time, so I got to watch the healing process from a different perspective, just as a bystander (she's like me and was trying to do far too much too soon – so I was forever bossing her around and getting her back on the sofa). What I learned is that whichever way our babies come out, our bodies have gone through something monumental and need time to recover and recuperate. It's difficult to sit and do nothing, to let others help out and admit we need their generosity, but please just do it. Because the sooner you do, the sooner you'll be outside in the sunshine eating that ice-cream. More importantly, the sooner you give in, the sooner you'll hold your baby in your arms without that deflating feeling of being raw, swollen and bruised. Soon enough none of that will register, and you'll just be there with your longed-for bundle, happily breathing in their beauty as though nothing existed before that moment.

7

TO BOOB OR NOT TO BOOB? THAT IS THE QUESTION!

TO BOOB OR NOT TO BOOB?
THAT IS THE QUESTION!

I think breastfeeding is one of those topics that I've really turned to others to suss out their opinion on before discovering my own thoughts. One friend asked me if I was going to try it (it's a question that seems to be asked by everyone, from friends and acquaintances to random male strangers in the supermarket). I was only seven weeks pregnant at the time and hadn't thought past the fact that there was a human growing inside me. I hadn't started planning anything for the baby's actual arrival, let alone thought about how I was going to keep them alive and fed. When I said I wasn't sure she told me she hadn't done it and had known from the start she wasn't going to. Her reasoning was that she'd just given the baby her body for nine months and was keen for it to be hers again. I understood where she was coming from and nodded in response. It was a fair argument. However, the conversation made me look into the matter a little more.

I went to the font of all knowledge, the internet – a useful tool that was soon to become my best friend when pondering the silliest of questions (like, *How loud should you play white noise for a baby?* or, quite simply, *Why is my baby still crying?*).

I hadn't been ready for the judgmental bashing that I was about to discover at the click of a button. In my naivety I hadn't realised breastfeeding was a subject up for such passionate debate. There seemed to be so much anger surrounding the matter. Anger that women were using their boobs for anything other than showing off their cleavage on a Friday night, anger that a mother would try and feed her baby naturally while sitting somewhere comfortable (apparently the toilet seat is more than adequate for that sort of monstrous behaviour, according to AngryManFromMars345), anger that some women would choose not to nurse their children (neglect at the first hurdle), and anger that people were putting anything other than breast milk into their babies. Anger, anger, anger. Just reading the remarks filled me with anxiety. I think it was the first time I really discovered how much judgment was associated with motherhood, and that people had such strong opinions on what they felt was wrong or right.

Then a dear friend of mine told me her own breastfeeding story. She'd tried her best to get along with breastfeeding. She really had. She was determined that the boob was the way she was heading. However, it really didn't work out well for her and her daughter. Something wasn't quite right and the latch was never comfortable. But my friend kept going with it, to the point where she still (five years later) had the scars on her boobs from sores and blisters. She had ample milk, but her daughter just couldn't work out her equipment, no matter how many midwives and people in the know grabbed hold of her baps and looked at what she was doing.

My disappointed friend was about to give up (I mean, how much did her boobs have to suffer?) when a midwife gave her a stern warning about the perils of formula, saying she'd be giving her daughter the equivalent of one hundred Mars Bars in her first year by making the switch. It was the old 'breast is best' campaign (and I'm pretty sure a completely made-up fact). My friend was mortified and so turned to expressing. She fed her daughter exclusively on expressed milk for six months, choosing to have someone else bottle-feed her child while she expressed the next feed in another room. Now, from experience I can say that I love expressing, but I'm sure my friend would rather have spent that time bonding with her child than feeling emotionally blackmailed into having a relationship with her breast pump, and resentful that someone else was experiencing the joy of feeding her daughter while she sat there feeling like a cow (at least that is how I can sometimes feel when expressing).

Anyway . . . all this made me think of my own views on breastfeeding and wonder if I actually had any. If I'm entirely honest I used to be quite shy around people feeding in front of me, even if they were my best friends. Not because I felt what they were doing was wrong or disgusting or something I didn't want to see – I'm not one of those twerps – but because I didn't know where to look and didn't want to be rude. I'd know there was a boob on the loose and didn't want my eyes to suddenly land on it and then be caught looking, because, let's face it, it's all pretty fascinating stuff and if you tell yourself not to look at something then you're most definitely going to. So I knew the whole thing made me a little uncomfortable, but not because I disagreed with breastfeeding, more because of my social awkwardness.

Another thing I wondered about was the actual getting my boobs out in public thing. I'm not a prude, but I wasn't a fan of that idea. I mean, it was fine for others to do, but my boobs were . . . well, mine. I also developed this bizarre fear of someone taking a picture of me while I was breastfeeding and uploading it onto the internet. I know – bonkers. Who'd do such a thing, let alone want to see it?! How self-centred am I? Well, we're all human, and we all suffer from the occasional irrational thought. OK – more than 'occasional' when preggers!

I sat on the breastfeeding fence for a little while without making any firm decisions. That said, the old 'breast is best' argument (which we've all heard bandied about time and time again) did tally with my desire to be the bestest mummy that ever existed, so I guess I was leaning more pro the idea than I realised. I just had to get my head around certain aspects of it (i.e. public bare-boobed-ness).

When I discovered hypnobirthing and found a profound love for my body and all its amazingness, I became more set on breastfeeding. I was determined to try and give it a bash; I even went to a class on it (I'm such a swot!). One of the midwives at the hospital mentioned she gave one-to-one sessions and I thought, why not? My main concern, though, was that I was going to get there and have to whip out a bap (or both) so that she could inspect them and see if they were up to the job. Like I've already protested, I'm not a prude, but I've never been the most confident when it comes to my body and I truly cringed at the thought of revealing so much of myself (a thought that is hilarious to me now after two natural births – I couldn't have cared less who saw what in that delivery room, especially during round two).

My teacher was a lovely, fun and bubbly woman from New Zealand. She walked me through the science bits and explained the art of getting it all right. It sounded so easy that I couldn't understand what the fuss was about. Get the baby into the desired position, tease him so that he opens his mouth nice and wide and then, with your boob shaped like a burger (sounds weird, but makes sense when you see it), wait for the optimum moment and then draw the baby in with as much breast in his mouth as possible. Easy peasy, lemon squeezy! I was even taught a variety of positions that might work should I feel the need to explore.

That was it.

I was ready.

I knew I wanted to get Buzz on the breast as soon as possible. I'd been told how important that would be and how he'd probably (in a fairy tale) sniff the boob out and get going of his own accord. Just as that ideal moment was about to happen in the delivery room (I don't think it actually was, but it could've done had I had more time) I heard a commotion in the corridor . . . Buzz's excited grandparents (both sets) had somehow blagged their way up through security and were on their way in to us. It wasn't the best start to our amazing breastfeeding journey, but seeing those four giddy grins and tears of joy as they passed Buzz around was enough for me to forget about it. And so I tried again a little later on, realising that Buzz was going to need to start his intake of nutrients. I took him to the boob and . . . nothing. I think he even stayed asleep. He wasn't bothered by it at all. I was majorly worried that I'd missed the window of opportunity – that the boob boat had well and truly sailed, and crashed into a tin of formula.

The midwife got me to keep trying, but Buzz really wasn't bothered. If he did get on he'd sit there with my nipple in his mouth for a bit but not do much with it, other than making me feel like a total – forgive the pun – tit.

You see, the problem was that although I'd had a class on breastfeeding and could easily talk through what I should've been doing, it was nothing like being faced with the real thing. Yes, I had a checklist of correct holds and what-have-you – but neither of us actually knew what we were doing. Breastfeeding can be explained in the simplest of terms, but it's pretty difficult to convey your seemingly straightforward desires to a fresh little newborn who's already shell-shocked by their new surroundings.

That's where we got stuck and when my boobs became everyone's property. Every midwife that came in to see us got a hold of them and tried to show me the correct way of getting him to latch on. One even gave me my first experience of hand-expressing, while collecting the tiny amount of colostrum that came out into a syringe. I mean, I'm sure I could've managed it myself, but I just sat there looking at her gormlessly when she gave me the instructions on what to do, so she offered to help. By that point I really didn't mind a hands-on approach and quickly realised the midwives had seen it all before. We then gave the tiny amount of colostrum to Buzz and he gobbled it up instantly, apparently loving it. I felt happy that I'd been able to give him something, but disappointed that it hadn't gone as well as I'd hoped. I knew I'd been doing my homework, but Buzz had obviously missed the How to Suck from a Boob class while in utero. He just wasn't playing ball, but while it was frustrating, I understood. I wasn't the only one who didn't really know what I was doing. The only difference was that he could get away with his cluelessness, whereas I felt a huge pressure to get it right and stop being such a plonker.

And so we kept going with the hand-expressing and syringe. I was then warned about getting him into bad habits (even though it hadn't been my idea to start with) and encouraged to persevere with trying him on the boob.

Nope.

Nothing.

Wondering whether it was my nipples he was having issues with, the lactation consultant at the hospital suggested trying with shields – essentially a plastic barrier shaped like a cone, which is easier for little ones to deal with. They helped keep him on there for longer, but I was then warned by a different midwife about shields being another bad habit. Argh! Next I was advised to express after a feed (for no longer than fifteen minutes) to help with my milk supply, especially if Buzz wasn't spending much time on the boob. It was all a kerfuffle and left me quite hot and sweaty every time we tried, but I so wanted to try. I don't know what it was but I suddenly felt like I really wanted it to work. I really wanted to be able to feed my baby. It became a huge desire of mine. I was no longer on the fence when it came to what I wanted to do. Breastfeeding was my chosen method.

As things still weren't running smoothly by the time we took Buzz home I was given the number of a recommended lactation consultant called Beth who I could pay to come and visit me at home and give me some more guidance. I knew I'd had conflicting reports on what to do at the hospital but seeing as Beth was a specialist on the matter, I called her up straight away. She was the sweetest lady – full of encouragement and support. She came out to see us the following day and was on hand for the next week via the phone as and when I needed her. Every day she'd arrange a time to call (which could be changed if we were mid-drama or meltdown), or check in towards the end of the day to see how I was getting on – not just in terms of feeding, but also emotionally and practically.

Beth got me to start making a note of feed times, how long they took and which boob was used – which I needed, because it was all becoming one big blur.

I must say that the midwives at the hospital were absolutely great, but I got the impression with Beth that she was totally on my side – and I hadn't even known I was up against anything in the first place. She just understood the chaos of having a newborn and the feeling of finding yourself totally dumbfounded by the simplest of tasks. She wasn't horrified at the sight of the nipple shield, although she eventually started suggesting I lose it mid-feed, just to see what would happen. From her it didn't seem like such a big deal.

I remember one night Beth phoned to check in and I just started crying (I told you I cried lots). I'd had a rubbish day. Buzz wasn't taking the boob without the shield, my nipples flipping hurt and we'd got hardly any sleep the night before – you know, normal new mum stuff. I can recall Tom being upstairs with Buzz and me sitting in my office sobbing on the phone. She just listened. She was kind like that. I know her kindness made me cry even more, but I also knew I needed the release. I needed to get out the emotions that were swirling around inside me like a mini-tornado. I didn't need to pretend with her.

It made me realise how important it is as a new mum to have someone there to just listen to you – and maybe that's the joy of having a near-stranger at the end of the phone, rather than having someone physically in front of you. It can almost be like you're thinking out loud and you don't feel the need to censor yourself quite so much. Beth was just so empathetic. She *knew*. She just *knew*.

The kindest thing Beth said to me in my overwhelmed state was to make a mental list of things I felt needed doing, but only try to do one of them – and then to rejoice in that achievement. The world wasn't going to end if I didn't get the washing done, people weren't (hopefully) going to think I was rude if I didn't get thank-you cards out straight away, and there was no rush to unpack my hospital bag – or even to get dressed in the mornings if I didn't feel like it on that particular day. I needed to stop putting so much unnecessary pressure on myself.

I heard her words.
They were a relief.
Although that doesn't mean I listened!
Sorry, Beth!

8
OH, HELLO, BABALONS!

OH, HELLO, BABALONS!

A few nights after Buzz was born I found myself feeling really poorly, almost like I had a virus, so I went to have a little lie-down. Lying there in the dark the weirdest sensation washed over me. This is going to sound crackers, but I felt small, weak, curled and fragile. In my mind I was newborn Buzz, squirming at the alien world around me. I was hallucinating. Then I became super cold and started shaking. Tom thought the sleep deprivation had finally got to me when I told him, but we phoned my doctor (I promise this was the last time I called him) and he reassured me that it was just my milk coming in and that it wouldn't last very long.

I was dubious over his diagnosis. I couldn't see how some milk going to my boobs would cause such a huge reaction within the rest of my body. It had to be something else. Nope. I didn't have to wait long to see that he was completely right. I woke up in the night to find two hard boulders strapped to my chest. And that's not an exaggeration. It was like they weren't a part of me any more, or like I'd had a botched boob job where the skin had stretched so much it became shiny and incredibly itchy. They looked ginormous, were rock solid and hurt like hell. And they leaked. Everywhere. I had been wondering whether I'd even need the breast pads I'd bought that were still neatly packed in my hospital bag, but the answer was a definite yes!

Getting out of the shower was the worst. I'd be in a race to see if I could get into my bra (which I would set out with pads already in before getting into the shower) before my boobs started squirting or dripping. I didn't always make it.

Talking of showers and breastfeeding, I must say that for the first few months after having both boys, I stank. I literally ponged within a minute or two of getting out of the shower. It was something I could never get my head around. How could I possibly smell like I'd run twenty marathons when all I'd done was step out of the bathroom and walk straight downstairs into the kitchen? I also had a permanent sweat on and could never tell what temperature a room was – which was a nightmare when trying to decide what to dress Buzz in.

My milk coming in made things even harder with Buzz and feeding. Because now if he took his time latching on he'd get a big squirt in the face – as though my let-down could sense that he was so close and couldn't wait to transfer the goods across.

Talking of let-down – no one tells you of the burning, tightening sensation that comes when a feed is due. The discomfort that comes with the beginning of a feed is also a little bit of a taboo. I was told continuously, and read over and over again, that if I was experiencing any pain when Buzz started feeding, he wasn't on correctly, and I should pop in my little finger to break the suction and start all over again. (Side note – how amazing is the little finger looped into their mouth trick? It's far better than trying to pull them off and subsequently stretching your nipples by six inches when they stubbornly keep going for it!)

A friend messaged me when I'd just given birth and mentioned how she used to kick her heels back into her chair at the start of each feed. At the time I had no idea what she meant, but I soon learned. Tensing my butt and curling my toes (sometimes even clenching my jaw) were my chosen methods to get me through. Not for the whole feed, mind. Just for that first blast, when they're so keen and hungry, and your body knows it – expelling that milk with great gusto.

I can remember going to a wedding when Buzz was ten weeks old and talking to a couple of friends who were also breastfeeding. I mentioned to them about still experiencing pain (as if everything I'd read had been wrong) and they looked at me like I was crazy. Neither of them were having this problem. That got me worried. Surely I wasn't the only one to feel that way, even if it was only at the start of each feed. Half of me wanted to seek help, but then the other half realised we had a good thing going. Buzz was putting on weight fast, so I knew he was getting enough from me, and I didn't want to do anything that might change that. Funnily enough, every time I went to get Buzz weighed (something I did weekly with Buzz but not even monthly with Buddy – I could see he was gaining weight and that was enough to let me know he was thriving) the midwives were always shocked that he was exclusively breastfed. It wasn't that he was ever a chunky baby, but compared to his tiny birth weight, he was solid – something that led them to assume he was formula fed. Go boobs! Yes, we were doing well as a team, so I didn't want to break something that didn't need fixing. I was happy to continue curling my toes and squeezing those butt cheeks a little longer!

I wouldn't say breastfeeding ever secured the bond between me and either of my boys, though. In fact, I'd say it almost went the other way with Buzz and it's something I really regret. It felt like everyone else got to hold him when he was peaceful, asleep and looking adorable, whereas I got my time with him when he was hungry and painfully attacking my boobs, or simply crying out of frustration.

When the feeds eventually started being successful in those early days, I'd sit feeding him for over an hour, then spend another hour trying to wind him and get him to go back to sleep, something that didn't feel too great in the early hours of the morning when I was absolutely shattered. Looking back now I wish I'd have just gone with it and enjoyed those little moments of us being up in the night together. I think I did sometimes, but I was distracted by the fact that I was so desperate for him to feed from the boob. I wish I'd have been a little more relaxed about the whole thing – although in those early days I had my own recovery to contend with, so it wasn't just the feeding situation I was up against.

I can remember packing for the McBusted tour, when Buzz was six weeks old, while speaking to Emma on the phone. I was getting all emotional (as per usual at that time) about the feeding situation and she asked why I was putting myself through it. I honestly didn't have an answer other than the fact that I'd had my mind set on it and didn't want to go back on that. Then she simply said to me, 'Gi, if it's making you unhappy, just stop.' Well, that shut me up – and not in a way that meant I couldn't moan or vent if I wanted to, but just in the sense that Emma had taken all the other crap away and put it so plainly. That's why she's flipping ace. If I was finding it so difficult and draining, if it was affecting my ability to mother, I should just stop. There was no point in torturing myself. I think someone just allowing me the option made me feel a little lighter. If I wanted to, I *could* stop. Bizarrely, I felt like stopping hadn't been an option before that.

I was just about to head to Manchester, where Buzz and I were spending two weeks together in a hotel while Tom and the boys went and did their thing up north (Tom was planning on travelling to and from there to various locations). We faced two weeks away from chores and all responsibilities other than looking after Buzz, just like it had been in hospital with him when we were both recovering from our infections – the difference being that this time I was fit and well and able to walk around (within reason). I wanted to make the most of having that time together, and being a short walk away from the city centre – not having to worry about cars or any other travel logistics.

That was it.

Our make-or-break boob vacation.

9

TOUR WITH A NEWBORN

TOUR WITH A NEWBORN

Whenever I'd tell people about going on tour they'd quickly suck air through their teeth, making that little hissing sound that automatically fills you with doubt and concern, and making me wonder whether I was doing the right thing. It was the reaction I got from everyone, but then I'm not sure what those people thought touring was actually like. I assume they must've thought we'd be travelling up and down the country, surrounded by drugs and alcohol, and going to loud rock and roll venues, but in reality we stayed in one hotel (The Lowry – I love it), are all grown up and sensible (half the band are now completely teetotal), and Buzz and I hardly ventured to the venues.

It was the first tour where I wasn't particularly bothered about being part of the band entourage – contrary to popular belief backstage isn't the most glamorous of places, neither is it home to many crazy antics (perhaps I shouldn't admit that). It's quite a chilled-out affair with soundcheck, physiotherapy and catering – the boys are always busy preparing for the show so you can end up feeling like a spare part if you're there too long, because everyone else there has a job and a purpose. No, Buzz and I were happy to stay at the hotel where we had the freedom to do as we wished. We were only on tour so that Tom didn't have to spend too long away from his son. I was just happy to comply with two weeks of housekeeping and having my food cooked for me. Unfortunately we did end up coming back with two weeks' worth of washing (have you seen how much hotel laundry services cost?!), but that was easy enough to sort through.

Talking of washing and packing, I took so much stuff with me. I chuckle at the thought of it. I took our SnuzPod (Buzz's crib) with us in case he didn't like the hotel cot, a Moses basket (although I'm not sure why), my rented hospital-strength breast pump (Medela Symphony) to ensure I stayed on top of those feeds and kept up my milk supply (I wasn't ready to switch to my normal pump, so clung on to this one for as long as I could), my steriliser, BabyBjörn bouncer, his play gym . . . honestly, it was a little ridiculous. Clothes-wise Buzz was also on the cusp of growing out of his newborn clothes (major sob), so I also had to pack some of his 0–3 months pieces too. Oh, and I should also mention that Buzz was one of those babies who always peed all over everything when he was being changed and whose poos were always of the explosive and leaky variety. He needed a lot of clothes to see us through the trip, so we basically took his whole wardrobe.

I thoroughly enjoyed our stay in Manchester. Having that time to just focus on us as a little family (other than when Tom went off for a gig) was priceless. I was able to get Buzz into a nice little sleep and feed routine, and on the whole he seemed a lot happier (apart from the occasional disaster – which I'll elaborate on later . . .). It was great for us to have a little more structure, too. We had just started our *Game of Thrones* obsession, so we were working our way through the first few seasons of that when Buzz slept. I was concerned the dramatic intro music and the violent scenes might have a psychological effect on Buzz, though, so we used to keep the volume quite low. Eventually we upgraded to using headphones with a splitter – BEST INVENTION EVER! I highly recommend them when travelling with children, especially if they're tucked up in their cot asleep and you want to bosh a box set or watch a film. Plus the one I found was less than a fiver on Amazon. Total bargain.

• • • • •

There were two nights of the trip where I was supposed to be at the hotel alone (Tom and the boys were playing and staying in Cardiff but it didn't make sense for us to move around when we were settled), but instead my brother Mario came up to stay with us.

I'd definitely say that having children in the family has made Giorgina, Mario and me a lot closer. I think a large part of that is how comfortable we are around each other. I know I can be myself around them. At that time in particular, when I was venturing into a new chapter of life, I felt I didn't have to put up any sort of pretence or act like I had everything under control. I knew I could be grumpy if I felt like it.

I knew I could have a good cry (there was one night, a week into my motherhood adventure, where I just broke down in sobs in front of them). Plus, those two crazy cats are the funniest people I know, always ready to offer a little light relief. I love them more than ever now.

Sibling admiration aside, let's get back to Manchester.

I was happy Mario was coming up to stay with us. He decided to treat us to a posh dinner at one of his favourite restaurants, Rosso. Now, I know what you're thinking: 'Are you mad, going out with a newborn?!' Well, by this point Tom and I had ventured out for a couple of meals with the other McBusted guys, so I felt like taking the plunge. Plus, I'd heard so much about the Italian restaurant from Mario that I found myself really looking forward to it. I gave Buzz a huge feed in the hope that it would buy us a solid three hours of him asleep in his pram.

It started well. As hoped, Buzz was asleep upon arrival – allowing me to take in the gorgeous decor, eat a few olives and enjoy being entertained by some Rat Pack classics being sung by a male crooner. Yep. It was delightfully atmospheric . . . so delightful, in fact, that Buzz felt he wanted to join in the fun. But he didn't just wake up. Noooo . . . he woke up and wailed. And wailed . . . and wailed. Ha! Mario had to chop up my dinner for me so that I could juggle eating with just a fork and bouncing Buzz in my other arm while we waited for the milk to heat up. The only blessing was that the music was loud enough to drown out his cries. Even though I don't think we ruined anyone else's dinner, I still got a serious case of mum sweats at being out in public with a crying baby – why, oh why couldn't I keep a newborn happy twenty-four seven?

Well, the whole thing was repeated again the following week when I decided to take Tom back to Rosso when he had a night off. The first week away had helped me gain more and more confidence at being out and about with Buzz, and I quickly learned to just do, not question. If I thought of going out for a walk, I just did it. No planning or procrastination. Just up and go. Otherwise I would talk myself through all the things that might go wrong and stress over it all.

It started off better than the previous time, with Buzz staying asleep during the starters and even the mains . . . and then he woke up demanding a feed. Even though we knew the cause of his mini-meltdown and were on it straight away, we still needed to calm him down while we heated up his milk.

He wasn't happy about the wait.

And he wanted everyone in the restaurant to know about it.

While we were tending to him I was aware of the two women sitting next to me looking over and making little comments to each other. I couldn't hear what was being said, but I felt my blood run cold as I filled in the blanks. I was certain they were questioning our parenting skills. I mean, who in their right minds would take a newborn to a fancy restaurant? Cue the mum sweats as I clenched my jaw and felt my face go bright red, my inner voice reciting the words 'they think you're a shit mum' on repeat.

A little while later, after Buzz had downed his milk, burped and gone on to do an explosive poop, one of the ladies turned around and said how gorgeous he was. Having been convinced they were both annoyed with us, I was caught off guard. I apologised for all the noise he'd made earlier. She laughed in return, gave a little shrug and said, 'Children cry.' Those words have stayed with me ever since. Yes, children cry. Of course they do. It's their main form of communication for a little while. But putting that realisation aside, her comment made me understand something else, too, and that was that not everyone outside my house was against me. Some (perhaps most) were actually looking on with encouragement and support. It was a pretty lovely discovery.

• • • • •

It seemed like Buzz really wanted to hammer home the point 'children cry' while in Manchester. Izzy was also up there for the tour, and halfway through the trip Emma came up with her children. We had a cosy night of room service planned while the boys were out playing a gig. Buzz had other ideas though. He cried and cried and cried and cried. He refused his bottle AND the boob, wouldn't burp, had a dry nappy, refrained from sleeping . . . he wouldn't calm down at all, no matter what I tried. He just kept going. All three of us ladies tried everything. Emma pulled out all her wise mum knowledge, and Izzy took him on a walk through the corridor while singing him lullabies. We kept passing him around, each of us trying a different calming tactic.

None of it was good enough.

After two hours of us trying our damnedest to appease his distressed state I took him back to our room. He suddenly stopped crying, had his bottle and was fast asleep by the time Tom came into the room five minutes later. He looked incredibly angelic and peaceful, as though he hadn't made a peep all night. So much so that Tom didn't believe me when I told him what had happened.

So yes, Buzz went through a period of being a little crier. Tom's mum Debbie says that Tom was the same when he was younger, and unfortunately Buddy has been too (although he's now coming out of it). For a while that made me worry about taking Buzz out, but encounters like the one I had with the lady in the restaurant encouraged (and continue to encourage) me to push myself further and to venture out. It doesn't matter if they cry, especially if I'm actively trying to resolve the situation. Plus, if they do have a meltdown here or there, then I try (it doesn't always work) to focus on the task in hand and not what some stranger might be thinking of me. I tend to feel calmer for blocking them out and am able to deal with the situation a lot more swiftly.

10
GETTING MY BAPS OUT
(AKA FEEDING IN PUBLIC)

GETTING MY BAPS OUT
(AKA FEEDING IN PUBLIC)

The other thing I really loved about being up in Manchester was that I would manage to feed Buzz in the room, go out for a little meander around the shops, or write out the never-ending thank-you cards (I did eventually get round to doing them after six weeks, but didn't do the same after having Buddy – OOPS) while sitting in Starbucks, and still get back in time for another feed. Yes, I was all about feeding indoors where I could get my boobs completely out and not have to worry about retaining my modesty. I just didn't want the added hassle of faffing with clothes when Buzz and I were still figuring out what we were doing. Plus I was still leaking everywhere.

Funnily enough, though, I was walking back from the shops one afternoon and I thought to myself, I'm just going to go to Costa and feed him there. It was the first time I can remember feeling relaxed about it. The thought was uplifting and empowering. About ten seconds after I made that decision (not even an exaggeration) a stranger called out to me, came over and started talking to me about Buzz. I didn't know the man, but he knew me from our videos and online posts. He was incredibly pleasant and lovely, but I didn't feel quite so cocky about my public feed then, and the irrational thought resurfaced of someone posting a photo on the internet of me with a milky boob hanging out and milk squirting water-gun-styley around the coffee shop. Sadly I went back to the room and fed Buzz there as previously planned.

· · ● · ·

I can remember one of the midwives telling me it took two weeks to properly establish breastfeeding. That was the kindest thing she could've told me. It gave me hope. It let me know that I wasn't the only one who struggled with something I'd always assumed was easy – after all, it's a natural thing to do, so how could it possibly be that difficult? Well, it blooming was and I found it encouraging to know it didn't come easily for everyone.

I try never to compare myself to other mums, but sometimes it can't be helped. Especially if I'm comparing in an area I might feel I'm failing in. Knowing about that two-week establishment period gave me a bit of relief. It did get a little better in that time, but in all honesty it probably took us about eight weeks to properly get to grips with the whole thing, and then at three months we experienced a magical boob moment of everything falling into place. I can remember sitting down on the sofa to feed Buzz, him latching on and then me realising it all felt completely different. His mouth was open wider and his lips were creating a better suction. The whole thing was far quicker (less than ten minutes compared to half an hour), easier and there was no discomfort at all. I'm not sure whether he'd found a more efficient way of working, or whether the fact he was a lot bigger and more capable meant he could just handle my boobs a bit better, but it was a drastic and sudden change. We had become a magical boob team just like that. I was so chuffed with how far we'd come from those early days in the hospital – back then it had seemed like a huge weight, an almighty challenge. Well, there we were conquering it.

Before giving birth I'd told myself I wanted to breastfeed for six months, or until Buzz got teeth. It's obvious why the gnashers would make me stop, but I didn't really have an explanation for the length of time, other than that it sounded like a good effort. By the time the six-month mark was approaching, though, I realised I wasn't done. I wanted to carry on, largely because the early days had been so emotional, traumatic and painful and now it was the opposite. It was easy and quick, something I never thought it would be. So I decided to plough on. A year was a nice round figure to aim for, but it still depended on those teeth arriving.

Before I came to the decision to keep breastfeeding, I saw photos online of gorgeous Olivia Wilde breastfeeding her baby during a photo shoot for *Glamour* magazine. She looked every inch the movie star with her designer dress, high-heeled shoes and immaculate hair and make-up, yet her focus is on the most grounding role any woman will ever have, being a mum. We see half an exposed breast (probably no more than we'd see on some red carpets or in music videos – no nipple or areola in sight) and the back of her naked baby, his bottom tastefully covered up. In fact the whole image is tasteful and elegant, as though she's on a break from the shoot and the photographer just happened to take the shot. Obviously I know that wouldn't have been the case – the image would've been carefully orchestrated with hair and make-up standing close by and a production runner poised with a towel at the ready, just in case the little boy had an eruption from either end, but it's such a stunningly beautiful, bold and brave photograph: almost a piece of art. It touched me and had me intrigued, yet it was the comments from readers on the website I was on (one known for its trolling) that really grabbed my attention. They were shocking, with people saying it was disgusting, that women shouldn't 'flaunt' themselves in that way and that breastfeeding in public was 'unnecessary'.

Now, I'd seen comments like these when I first thought about breastfeeding, but now that I was doing it myself I couldn't believe what I was reading.

I was livid.

I couldn't comprehend the attitude some people had towards a baby being fed by his mother. It was about far more than just the picture. It spoke volumes on us as a society. There were adults suggesting mothers take their babies into the toilet to feed them . . . really? Now, I've admitted that I had previously been a little awkward when confronted with a bare-boob feeder, and I know I couldn't personally do that myself, but I would simply choose not to look if it angered me that much! Plus, that woman who's sitting with a baby at her breast is feeding her child – not coming on to you sexually! Perhaps the fact that many people automatically associate boobs with sex is the problem when it comes to breastfeeding.

I was pretty outraged and sent a few angry tweets before removing myself from my computer so I could calm down.

I found myself annoyed that I'd spent months locked away

indoors, working my outings around feed times or nipping back to the car quickly so that I didn't have to inconvenience anyone else. But what about the inconvenience I was causing to my hungry child?

The next day we were in Bath and Buzz was due a feed. I was going to go back to the car to do it, but then stopped myself. We were out in a beautiful quiet park and the sun was shining gloriously. I was ready for my first public breastfeeding experience. I wasn't going to be told what I could and couldn't do when it came to the welfare of my child. So in a mini-protest I sat on a park bench in the shade, wrapped a big swaddle blanket over my shoulder and fed my baby al fresco. It was pretty liberating and terrifying at the same time. I kept looking around to see if anyone had noticed, whether they were going to come at me with a tirade of abuse, but no one did. It was a peaceful protest with a peaceful outcome. I was so giddy I got Tom to take a picture of me so I could share it online. Why? Because after months of struggle there I was, surrounded by nature, doing something utterly natural.

Funnily enough, once I posted it, I then got a few messages from mums who were disgruntled that I was covering him up with the swaddle, but as I've said, it's my body and I'll do what I feel comfortable with. I hate the feeling of being judged, but, rather sadly, I've found that's a huge part of being a mum. And even though I have exclusively breastfed both of my boys I still feel the judgment when I pull out a bottle of expressed milk. It's probably entirely in my own mind and an anxiety I'm putting on myself, but I always wonder if people think I'm giving them formula (this has led to me using only Medela bottles, simply because they're so heavily associated with breast-feeding). I also wonder if they think I'm ridiculous and vain for not just putting him on the boob when I'm right there with him . . . Argh! It's no good second-guessing strangers, or worrying what they think. If my baby is happy and feeding then it's not for anyone else to comment or even have an opinion on how I'm feeding him. And that's the thing, I think, especially when it comes to feeding: we're seeking approval from others for our decisions, but we don't have to. We don't need their acceptance to validate our own actions and decisions. We just need to understand our own reasons for the choices we make, and get on with it. That's something I've learned anyway, and for me that's where the phrase 'happy mum, happy baby' comes from. If you are miserable, in pain, depressed or anxious because you're trying to breastfeed your baby and it's just not working, then it's not only your milk your baby isn't getting. He or she is not getting the best of you at all. That's something I've only realised in hindsight, but it's something I'm really passionate about emphasising to new mums who might feel pressurised into fitting into other people's ideals, rather than doing what would make them comfortable and happy. And as my wise dad once said to me, you're the most important person in the world to your child – and your child deserves the best of his or her mummy. Your love and comfort is the most important thing you will ever give them – only a numpty would say otherwise.

· · • • ·

I frequently get asked in interviews my thoughts on celebrities posting pictures online of themselves breastfeeding their children. It's an awkward thing to be asked about because I never know what to say, but really it's just sad that it even merits a conversation; that it's such a 'shocking' thing for them to be doing. You could have the same celebrity sharing the same amount of flesh on a lingerie shoot and no one would bat an eyelid. We've sexualised boobs, which is fine – they're blooming gorgeous – but we also need to acknowledge that they're as great at multi-tasking as their owners are.

I feel that unfortunately, breastfeeding in public is a topic people will always clash on. I'd love breastfeeding to be some-thing that people have no reaction to whatsoever so that mothers can get on with it without feeling self-conscious about it, but I'm not entirely sure how we get there. Perhaps it's simply developing a greater understanding of those around us. For now I will just continue feeding respectfully when I'm out, and hope that whoever sees me will be just as respectful back.

My stance on public feeding shifted again when Buddy came along. At first I had the same nerves and concerns (I'd been out of the game for a year), but when you have a toddler running around you can't simply go back to the car for a feed, neither can you hibernate indoors without all getting cabin fever. You have to go out. You have to make plans. Only through doing it more and more have I started to feel increas-ingly comfortable with public feeding.

I still feel a little self-conscious feeding in front of male friends (not because I think they're looking, but simply because I have my boob out), but this time round I've just got on with it.

Something that has made it all far easier is the clothes I've been wearing (not a swaddle in sight). I'm all about the layering – one top going up while the other stays down, exposing only the necessary area. Now, there have obviously been times when Buddy hasn't played along with my discreet method and has chosen to repeatedly pull off, instead. The worst time this has happened (so far) was in the very early days when I was feeding him in a restaurant. My milk supply hadn't evened out yet and feeds were always a little slippery, but on this particular occasion when Buddy pulled away he did so with a big suck, meaning the milk continued to squirt out with great force. I don't know whether my male friend even realised. I was too red-faced to even address the situation or to look him in the eye for a minute or two . . . but then, what's a little squirted breast milk between friends?

· · · · ·

Personally, I always seem to feel a bit more normal and in control when I say goodbye to my breast pads. Don't get me wrong – I love them for keeping me dry (for the most part), but there's nothing flattering about having a panty-liner in your bra. Especially if you end up getting a cheap emergency pack from the nearest supermarket and spend the day rustling every time you move – hardly subtle, it feels like you're telling the world that you have a stuffed bra.

That being said, I've sometimes found it tricky to judge when is the right time to ditch the pad. Done too soon, you might find yourself with a little leakage problem – something that's happened to me both with my dad and my father-in-law. Pretty mortifying. Neither seemed to notice, but I definitely did.

Actually, I have suffered a more major leakage too. It occurred six weeks after Buddy was born – and I was wearing pads! We were heading into town for a business meeting, my post-partum physiotherapy session and for my six-week check. As we knew it was going to be a long day we decided to leave Buzz with Tom's mum (he'd have more fun with her), but take Buddy with us.

It was one of those rare days as the mum of a newborn when you wake up feeling refreshed, in control and like a total #mumboss. I'd had a chance to dry my hair properly, put some make-up on, and was finally out of my comfies/pyjamas – instead I was wearing a shirt-dress, leggings, boots and a blazer. I felt absolutely wonderful – and the feeling was increased ten-fold when Tom posted a picture of me on Instagram. Now, I know I need no man to validate my amazingness, but nonetheless, it made me feel like a desirable woman.

Life was great.

I was great!

Even with Buddy with us, we managed to bosh it through the first meeting with ease. The pair of us were managing baby-care while holding conversations and even eating. We were winning at life. Seeing as it was a breakfast meeting in a posh restaurant I'd chickened out of unleashing the boob and taken a bottle of expressed milk with me (total coward, but again, it's my body and all that . . .). I didn't express at that point or indeed at the end of the meeting, which, in hindsight, was where I made a serious error.

Buddy then had a feed a few hours later in a Starbucks while I sipped on a black coffee, appearing like I was totally owning the mumma-feeding-discreetly-in-public thing, and looking completely badass (even if I do say so myself).

However, at this point in time Buddy was a one-boob man. He didn't need the pair to quench his thirst. One did the job adequately. So after he'd had his fill my unwanted left boob remained untouched . . .

Not to worry, I thought. All is well. He'll want another feed soon enough.

So off we plodded to the hospital for physiotherapy (I was told off for not doing my pelvic floor exercises – something I always forget about even though I know I shouldn't unless I want to be wetting myself forever more), before heading in to see the midwives who'd been around when I delivered Buddy and had handled all the appointments and check-ups during my pregnancy.

They were a wonderful team of women who were incredibly supportive, kind and funny. What surprised me about this appointment was the ease of it. Ultimately they just wanted to check me over and see how I was doing, but they also wanted to talk about my birthing story – it seems they'd all been talking about it a lot and had enjoyed it as much as I had. So much so that my lovely midwife Roisin, who had been in the delivery room with us, told me I should write a book about the whole experience – dispelling the myths and reminding women how powerful our bodies are . . . I'm not sure this is quite that book, but I hope it'll still make her smile.

The midwives were really encouraging, and I felt completely empowered in their presence. There were lots of hugs and loveliness as we left – it was delightful.

It was only when we'd got into the lift to go downstairs that I realised I felt wet. Very, very, very wet. My left boob had leaked through my breast pad and all down my left side. Thankfully I had a patterned dress on, but my milk had caused the dye from my red bra to run down the white top I had on underneath. Eek! I was thankful the midwives hadn't seen it, and luckily I could cover it up with my blazer. I just felt a little damp for the remainder of the day – and a lot less sexy and empowered than I had earlier.

That particular night saw a meltdown and a poo in the bath (from one of the boys, not Tom or me!), so needless to say, the day ended less successfully than it had started. But that's motherhood for you. Each day is as varied and unpredictable as the next, as is each hour and minute. You can feel completely on top of things and then BOOM, it all goes to poop. But I like to savour those feelings of being in control as much as I possibly can – that way I don't feel quite so depleted when things fall apart. Having said that, it's amazing how quickly you move on. I've found I can't carry a downbeat mood with me. I've had to just accept the moment, perhaps put it away to laugh at later, and then move on.

11
THE NIGHTLY CHAOS

Newborn Buzz. Hard to think that delicate little flower is now running around the house creating such chaos.

He started it . . . then I carried on and drew him a little goatee. I did have a mini panic when the washable pen didn't come off instantly, but all was well.

Buzz helping mummy water some plants in the garden and looking incredibly cool in the process. I wish I could pull this look off!

That cheeky face . . . he's fully aware I'm about to shake the watering can in his direction and get him wet. Ooh, the suspense!

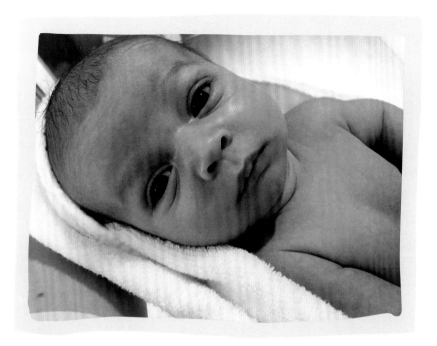

A freshly bathed Buddy looking alert and full of the wisdom. I'd love to know what he's thinking here. If I had to guess I'd say it was boob related.

Naked and on the move!

Snuggly days with Buzz.

My little hero. My silver lining.

At four months post-baby the tufts start to grow… I'm still waiting for them to calm down and integrate into the rest of my hair.

My thirtieth birthday – I had a delicious meal with family and friends. Tom and Buzz came matching. This happens a lot!

When we were three.

We have so many pictures like this – Buzz sat, full of love for his little brother, completely oblivious to the screams coming from Buddy.

A nice family photo at Tom's book launch for *The Christmasaurus*.

Me and my little bear Buzz.

One of Buzz's current obsessions is *Cars*. He also loves, or has loved, *Winnie the Pooh*, *The Muppets*, *The Little Mermaid*, *Oliver*, *The Snowman*, *Charlie and the Chocolate Factory*, *Finding Nemo* . . . the list is endless. His love of Lightning McQueen has been the most loyal.

Early morning cheekiness.

THE NIGHTLY CHAOS

When I was pregnant I was recommended a book called *The Sensational Baby Sleep Plan* written by Alison Scott-Wright. My friend had raved so much about it that I bought it instantly and added it to my reading pile of motherhood study guides. Around four weeks in, when Buzz simply wouldn't sleep (Tom was staying in the spare room because he had a cold and didn't want us to get it – so I was flying solo) and was demanding a feed every two hours, I read it. I felt broken, emotional and sore (well, my nipples did), and ready to try something new.

It was actually at this point I whipped out a dummy, too – just to give my baps a rest. Love them or loathe them, those devilish contraptions are called pacifiers for a reason – and as Buzz wouldn't settle unless he was on my boob I decided to see if a little diverted suckling would help him.

The dummy debate is one of those really divisive parenting topics. Before having children myself I hated the thought of dummies – perhaps having read too much negative stuff about them in the media – the implication always seeming to be that they are only given by lazy and neglectful parents who can't be bothered to adhere to their child's needs or try to appease them. I didn't want my baby sucking on some plastic and getting buck teeth when I just had to be a better mum . . . Hahahahahaaaa . . . The realities are always different to any judgmental nonsense that's usually fuelled by anything but fact and experience. Oh how ruddy wrong, foolish and gullible I was. It's shameful!

I have friends whose babies won't take a dummy, and they wish they would; on the other hand, I have friends who're relieved they've never had to resort to one and therefore saved themselves the judgmental comments. Anyway. I did, and Buzz blooming loved the dummy. I would usually only let him have it when he was due to go to sleep, so I guess it eventually became another signal of his routine and what was expected of him. Even though Buzz loved it, he didn't need it for very long, sometimes only for a minute before spitting it out and drifting off. All the same, I always had an emergency dummy in my bag when we went out, just in case he had a full-on meltdown. He started rejecting the dummy at around six months. In fact he'd cry until it was taken *out* of his mouth and then settle down to sleep.

We thought we'd got away with it with Buddy as he seemed far calmer, but then at eight weeks he had some major melt-downs and we decided to see if he just needed the comfort of a dummy. He did. I'd say Buddy had a dummy a little more in the daytimes than Buzz did – especially if other people were over and he made a noise – they'd see a dummy sitting there and just shove it in, whereas I like him to make some sounds and get used to his own voice. (At the point of writing this Buddy is eight months old and still has a dummy, but only when he's getting into his cot for a nap or bedtime. I no longer take emergency dummies out with me . . . I might regret that at some point.)

So, back to the sleep book. It was an informative read, but I'd already realised by that point that no two babies, or two mothers, are the same – and that I wasn't too keen on the sterner methods of parenting (especially for an innocent newborn who just craves your love). So instead of taking everything as gospel, I picked out the parts and ideas I liked and discarded the rest.

One of the main concepts I loved from the book was the introduction of a bedtime routine. We didn't quite follow what Alison Scott-Wright suggested; rather, we did a little variation on it. At four weeks, we introduced a bath at 9.30 p.m. followed by a bottle of expressed milk, which was given by Tom while I expressed in the other room. We then put Buzz into a white babygro (colours are for daytime madness, white is for night-time calmness) and lay him in his SnuzPod in our room at 10 p.m., rather than bringing him back downstairs with us (that's if we were going downstairs and not conking out in our own bed). The aim was to give Buzz a cuddle, lay him down and then allow him to self-settle, so that he wasn't reliant on us to help him drift off (it didn't always work, but we'll come to that later).

The first night we followed the new schedule Buzz managed to sleep a solid seven hours. SEVEN HOURS! I was so shocked when we woke up in the morning to see so much time had passed! I felt like a completely brand spanking new woman thanks to the extra hours of shut-eye. Honestly, I felt invincible.

It's crazy how refreshed something as simple as sleep can make you feel. That being said, I then found myself staring at Buzz and willing him to wake up pretty sharpish. My boobs didn't appreciate the night off. They hadn't got the memo and so had filled up with milk, far too much milk. They were sore, rock hard and massive! Literally aching to be relieved.

A short time after that sleep-filled night, less than two weeks later, as Buzz was taking to the routine so well, we decided to move the bedtime shenanigans forward to before the 7 p.m. feed – which was our ideal time for him to be going to bed. Well.

The first night we made the shift was awful. I've actually found a message I sent to a friend, whose own baby was just two weeks older than Buzz, which simply said, 'FYI . . . Last night was an epic fail! Up all night long.' I'd messaged her the night before about moving the bedtime routine forward, so I clearly felt I needed to share the outcome. Buzz was up continuously and seemed more unsettled than ever before – wanting more feeds again. It was knackering and frustrating. I tried my best, if he stirred, to let him try to sort things out for himself (waiting a few minutes before going to him) but it didn't always work and I felt cruel. I kept telling myself off, reminding myself of the old saying 'If it ain't broke, don't fix it', but it was done by that point. We just needed to keep going.

Our perseverance paid off eventually, and within a couple of days he was sleeping longer again – and not waking up for extra feeds. Our baby was finally sleeping from 7 p.m. through to roughly 6 a.m. I can't tell you how much of a relief that was.

I've got to say, though, having a sleeping baby can make

you feel so guilty! I would feel awful when we went to baby classes and other mums would share their stories of continuously being up with their babies who were far older than Buzz was. I could never bring myself to say that Buzz had turned into a great sleeper, because there's no way of saying that without sounding incredibly smug.

One mum has actually always stuck in my mind. Her little boy wasn't sleeping, but as she was telling us of the terrible night she'd had with him she was laughing hysterically. 'Yeah, he was up every hour last night. Ha, ha, ha. No sleep for us. Ha, ha, ha,' she chuckled with the manic desperation of a woman trying to keep her sanity while faced with torturous sleepless nights. Gosh, I felt for her. And I've thought of her every time we've had a little blip in our plans – because they do come. They're inevitable if the boys are poorly, teething or if there is a disruption to their routine. I always find those sporadic nights of no sleep worse than the early days of having a newborn actually – at least back then you sort of expected to get little sleep. When you're back in sleeping mode, to have it unexpectedly snatched away can leave you feeling like you've had the rug pulled completely out from under you – or the duvet pulled from over you.

We were lucky. Buzz was a great sleeper for the majority of the first year of his life. Only foolish parents would do something to jeopardise that . . . but more on that when I talk about our trip to Australia (seriously, trying to structure this book is such a challenge – I'm so used to my mum chats bouncing from one topic to another and then back again. Must. Stay. On. Track).

The bedtime routine helped all of us achieve a little structure in our days – something that had been lacking since Buzz arrived. It also meant that life on the road with Tom was a little easier, as Buzz had a regular plan that was familiar to him, and which we were able to stick to in hotels really easily. There was something quite luxurious about being in a hotel room while Tom was out at a gig and Buzz slept next to me. The peace was lovely!

The aforementioned sleep book also gave us some guidance on daytime naps – the only problem was that Buzz had his own ideas. When I look back I remember feeling like I spent the majority of my days trying to get him to nap during daylight hours (with all the aids – Ewan the sheep, a white noise app, a dummy, lots of rocking and shushing, pram outings, trips in the car) but he would just stare at me with a creased little frown, as though he knew what I was up to and wasn't best pleased.

When he did eventually do what was being asked of him, he would only sleep for thirty minutes. Precisely, usually. It was the oddest thing. So even when he was a year old he was having three, sometimes four, half-hour naps a day. It was crazy and I could never get a thing done – I know other mums who do all their chores and organise their lives in that mythical two-and-a-half-hour napping window. I barely had time to put a load of washing on or reply to emails. I had to really think wisely about what I chose to do and when. Sometimes I got it wrong, like the time on tour when I chose watching an episode of *Game of Thrones* over having a shower. A total error given the fact I was in my smelly breastfeeding mum of a newborn phase. I stank and regretted my choice for most of the day! Well, until I discovered the joys of a baby bouncer, that was. Buzz would sit comfortably in that and watch me have a shower. Honestly, sometimes simple gadgets like that which have been around the longest are magical. Thank you, BabyBjörn (and no, I'm not being sponsored).

It was only when we came back from a holiday and Buzz had a bit of jet lag that his middle nap became two hours and we were able to properly drop the others. It was as though his system had been rebooted. But by that time we were only a little way off Buddy arriving, so knew our life would be turned on its head again anyway.

Buddy is fab at his daytime naps. There was a time when he did the same as Buzz and became a lover of the thirty-minute cat nap, but thankfully he grew out of that quite quickly – especially if put down for a nap in his cot. He's been really good at self-settling, although it's not something I've consciously thought about, as I've been so focused on keeping Buzz in some sort of a routine and haven't wanted to rock the boat (Buzz has moved from the nursery into his big-boy bed). Buddy goes down nicely and doesn't cry.

You might think I've held him less because of having Buzz, but that's not true. I've held Buddy a lot. It was something I was really conscious of. All the books tell you to put your baby down to sleep so that you don't 'make a rod for your own back' – so that's what I did with Buzz. It was only when a friend of mine fondly referred to the 'sleepy cuddles' that her daughter had grown out of that I had a pang of regret, feeling once again like I hadn't made the most of having that precious time. That afternoon, after she'd mentioned it, I let Buzz fall asleep on me. Ahhh . . . It was absolutely wonderful. That fuelled my decision not to be so regimented and strict on myself this time round with Buddy. Not that I went totally the other way, but I was more relaxed. We were calmer parents in general, probably helped by the fact that Tom was home and we had two pairs of hands for the majority of the time.

Now that he's bigger, Buddy does go upstairs for his naps, but he gives the biggest smiles and hugs afterwards. He is always so pleased to see you when he wakes up. Night-time is slightly different. He is superb at going to bed. We do the same bedtime routine we did, and still do, with Buzz. He has a bath, bottle with a story (which we all read together) then one of us will take him into his room, read another short book or sing a little lullaby while giving him a cuddle, before putting him into bed.

Usually he babbles happily to himself for a minute or so before rolling over and drifting off. If only the rest of the night was that easy. Buddy was initially sleeping through until

5.30 a.m., having a feed and then going back to sleep until 7ish. Somehow that's regressed into him waking up at midnight, 3 a.m. and then 5.30 a.m. Saying that, he is snuffly at the moment, so maybe he's just having an off couple of weeks. I'm sure that by the time this is published he'll be back to sleeping through the night. Here's hoping!

I must say, though, there is something rather lovely about cradling your child in the dark of the night, knowing that the majority of the world outside is snoozing. I used to use feeding times to send emails, write a quick blog or text back a friend who'd been in touch – it seemed a great way to use that time considering both boys have fed with their eyes shut (I'd hate for them to look up at me and see my eyes just glued to a screen). But I've found something incredibly peaceful in those moments when I've had nothing to focus on but the task in hand. That's what the night feeds have become – largely because the glare from my screen burns my eyes so badly. It's something I'm thankful for; I cherish the closeness in those moments, and know I'll feel sad when I no longer have them.

12

WOMAN HAS BABY. WOMAN'S BODY CHANGES. WORLD GOES NUTS

WOMAN HAS BABY. WOMAN'S BODY CHANGES. WORLD GOES NUTS

Allow me to let you into a little secret: having babies changes your body! Whoooa! I know, I know. What an eye-opener. We've all heard the old chauvinistic 'like watching your favourite pub burning down' crap regarding the delicate foof area during childbirth (why don't men try shooting a lemon out of their winkle and then see if the joke is still funny), but it goes far further than having some weird metaphor attached to your genitals.

My body changing wasn't something I'd really considered before falling pregnant, because I was so consumed by the 'getting pregnant' part. That is to say, in my dreamlike fantasy of what building a family would look like, I'd thought about my body growing a baby and my body getting bigger during the pregnancy, but I hadn't given too much thought as to what would happen to it afterwards.

Someone else kindly put that thought into my head for me, though.

I was being interviewed a month before I was due to give birth to Buzz and was asked whether I had a plan to get back to my pre-birth shape when the baby arrived.

Come again?

You mean I wasn't going to be walking out of the hospital looking exactly like I had nine months previously? You mean people were going to be paying my post-partum body any attention when there was a gorgeous newborn around to coo over? Or, more pertinently, you mean I was meant to care and have a plan in place to obliterate the aftermath of birthing my unborn child before they'd even entered the world? Seriously?

I was a little dumbfounded about how to respond. I think I replied diplomatically along the lines of it not being something I'd thought about, but that I was looking forward to going for a walk without carrying around the excess weight of pregnancy. It was a pretty naff response to a question that made me wonder whether post-pregnancy weight was something I should start worrying about. Because here's the thing: when I was pregnant I experienced a newfound appreciation for the body I'd spent years hating. I'd look back at old pictures and think, Man, you were fine, not understanding why I'd been so mean about it before. I couldn't even see the supposed flaws that had previously caused me to be so crippled with insecurities. I'd wasted decades putting it down, stupidly focusing on the 'lumps and bumps' that were pretty much non-existent, because I thought it didn't compare well to the bodies of those around me. Bodies that I thought encapsulated so-called perfection better than my own.

When I was pregnant that all slipped away. And not just that, but I'd look at my growing pregnancy body (because it wasn't just the bump, it was the whole body – even my arms got in on the expanding action) and be in complete and utter awe of it. It was doing what it was created for, what so many women long for their bodies to do. It was growing an actual human, a mini-person to join forces with the next generation and, hopefully, fill our future with love and kindness.

Was I naive to not already have my workout routine in place? To not have signed up with a personal trainer and had him size up the damage so that he could set about making a plan to eradicate any signs that my body had undertaken such an arduous task?

It took a while for me to mull it over, but I eventually decided that everyone is different when it comes to pregnancy weight and the shifting (or not) of it. First things first, there's the whole exercise-in-pregnancy debate, with some loving the fact they're largely able to keep going with what they were doing before, and others packing it all in and deciding on a slower pace of life for a while. I have to say, I packed it all in. I wasn't even doing my favourite brisk early-morning walks for the first five months or so. From the minute I found out I was pregnant I stopped anything that might have been in the slightest bit challenging. Why? Because I'd miscarried during my first pregnancy. Because I was worried that if I overexerted myself it would happen again. Because I simply didn't want to risk it.

Now, you can tell me I'm foolish for thinking those things and tell me that studies have shown there's no link between exercise and miscarriage, but I don't really care. For me, at that time, I wanted to feel like I was doing as much as I could to ensure the safe arrival of my unborn child. And that meant taking it easy.

As things got further along with the pregnancy Tom and I did go for leisurely walks together and I started a weekly, very low-risk pregnancy yoga/meditation class (we barely moved), and I discovered a love of swimming in the slow lane (mostly because I felt so light and buoyant), but that was it. I felt safer introducing those bits towards the end of the pregnancy, when I knew I had to start preparing my body for labour, but the risks of losing our baby were becoming smaller. I breathed a huge sigh of relief at the 'viable' twenty-four-week mark, but still knew I wouldn't feel completely relieved until I had our baby in my arms. I felt the same way when I was pregnant with Buddy, regardless of the fact everything had gone smoothly with Buzz.

Even though I chose not to hammer it hard at the gym, it doesn't mean I have a negative opinion of those who do. As long as we're all looking after ourselves and our unborn children, then it's really no business of anyone else. We each know our own body's capability, and we have to listen to it if it tells us it wants us to do more or less.

That said, there is an obsession – yes, an obsession – with how much weight women put on in pregnancy (I've been asked for that figure in an interview before too) and I think it's a terrible shame and puts an emphasis on something we shouldn't be giving our attention to. Plus the context is a completely different one to that of normal weight gain – a woman hasn't just piled on a few stone in nine months for no good reason. For someone who hasn't had a baby or is nowhere near that stage in her life, the thought of possibly putting on up to five stone might be horrific, but it happens. For some, our bodies just take on a life of their own and it doesn't make a woman carrying a baby feel good to know she is being judged from all sides. I've had extremely slim friends who've (in their own words) ballooned during pregnancy due to water retention. And, for one friend, the negative and unwelcome attention she received from outsiders led her to be incredibly depressed during a time when she should've been ecstatic and full of excitement.

At around seven months into my pregnancy with Buzz I can remember seeing a big spread in a glossy magazine of a newborn photo shoot. It was a beautiful shoot and the new family had that lovely glow that I now recognise as being completely knackered but utterly in love with the new addition to their unit. However, it was the attached headline that caught my eye, stating that the new mum had only gained 6lbs during her entire pregnancy . . . How? Surely the baby alone weighed that much? And more than that, how had that turned into the main focus of the special moment the article was meant to be celebrating? It almost tells new mothers that that's what's expected of them – that putting on just a little weight should be something to be proud of. It's not. But neither is putting on too much weight. There should be no focus on the weight element as long as the mum is staying healthy and looking after herself! Instead, it should be on the wonderful thing their body has been able to achieve.

Anyway, it got me wondering how my own body was doing. I knew I felt a lot heavier and I had a nice-sized bump on display, so before going for a tasty dinner with Emma and Matt Willis, I decided to weigh myself. I'd put on two stone. I had a long way to go until the baby arrived and I felt this dread creep over me. How could the mother in the magazine have only put on a quarter of the weight I had and I wasn't even done growing yet? As soon as I saw Emma I told her of the scales and what they'd revealed. 'What the bloody hell did you do that for?' was her response, before telling me that it wasn't the right time to be worrying. And she was absolutely right. It's what I'd been thinking before, but having someone else say it validated my own thoughts somehow, or maybe just firmed them up. I love looking to others for a bit of guidance and reassurance – but I think it's important to turn to friends who have your best interests at heart rather than a stranger who just wants to comment because they feel they can, or a magazine that's wanting to captivate its readership with intriguing headlines.

When anyone's attention focuses on weight, be it gain or loss, and uses that observation to glorify some and belittle others, I feel my cage get rattled. And it's not a new thing we're contending with – the media has been inclined to comment on the blossoming and slimming of the female form for years. But having that focus on a pregnant woman's figure is concerning. Knowing how much I hated my own body growing up, and how comments and articles in magazines and newspapers used to feed into that hatred and those insecurities, I can't help but wonder how these comments might make new mums, women who are already under huge emotional stress with their hormone levels having gone haywire, feel. We're all human. I don't think I'll ever understand the need to judge others on their weight, but doing so after a body has given birth is plain wrong, in my opinion.

I also feel there's a huge 'us and them' culture growing regarding 'celebrity' mums and 'normal' mums. Aren't we all, first and foremost, simply mums? Why do we feel the need to add a label? In the media it seems a 'celeb' mum has either 'snapped back' (a phrase I abhor) into her pre-pregnancy jeans or is 'embracing her new curves'. How do the people behind such articles know this? How do they know it wasn't constant scrutiny from such articles that has led to a mother gym-ing it while her child sleeps, even though she desperately needs to lie down and sleep herself. How can they be sure the celebrity mum with the newfound curves hasn't had a terrible time adjusting to the change and is therefore constantly beating herself up? How do they know they aren't both battling postnatal depression and finding the whole thing overwhelming? How do they *know*?

Another question I get asked in interviews is 'Do you feel a pressure from celebrity mums to lose the baby weight straight away?' Call me crazy, but I don't think Megan Fox gives two hoots whether I get back into a pair of non-maternity jeans or whether I lounge around in my maternity joggers for the next six months. Instead I'm sure she feels a pressure from the people fixated on her weight and the studio who are employing her for her next role and expecting her to still look like Megan Fox – I'm not even going to pretend to know what that must feel like for her.

During my pregnancy with Buzz, I revelled in the fact that for the first time in my life I felt proud of the incredible, baby-growing, curve-filled body I was in. I didn't want to start planning an attack of punishing workouts when I was still living in my happy pregnancy bubble.

13

THE TALE OF THE JELLY BELLY AND OTHER BODILY WOBBLES

THE TALE OF THE JELLY BELLY
AND OTHER BODILY WOBBLES

was filled with pride and elation during my pregnancy with Buzz. Hit with utter awe at the magical qualities my body had been hiding from me all my life.

Then I had the baby.

Buzz was out in the world, but it seems my body didn't get the memo as it was still pretending to be pregnant. My bump was still there, parading itself around with continued delight. I was aware of it, of course, but between the gorgeous newborn I'd been blessed with and the stitches up my foof, it wasn't something I was too concerned about straight away. It was just my empty bump, the wobbly void that once held my baby.

Funnily enough, I'd never considered the term 'jelly belly' to actually be representative of anything real. Turns out I was wrong. My post-partum tum was *just* like jelly on a plate, and I became obsessed with touching it – like a newly shaved head of hair, it was just too intriguing to leave be. I needed to feel the softness of it every so often, my body continuing to surprise me with its new qualities, even then.

Bizarrely, I owe a big thank you to Kate Middleton here – and no, that isn't a name-drop, I've never had the pleasure of meeting her. However, if it hadn't been for the huge media frenzy she caused leaving the hospital after having Prince George with her cute little just-given-birth tummy on display in that pretty light blue dress, then I really wouldn't have known what to expect afterwards. Her doing so got people talking and, although I'm sure there will have been lots of judgmental comments flying around, I think she did every mother a favour by being seen in the immediate aftermath of childbirth. Whether she intended to or not, she showed the realities of giving birth, and sent a message to each of us, telling us, 'It's OK.' It's OK to step out in public straight after giving birth without hiding every trace of what our bodies have been through. More than that, though, Kate displayed her little bump with such affection, clearly still proud of her body and all it had given her. It was such an empowering image, and I thought about it after giving birth. It reminded me that I should still be in awe of my baby-making machine of a body even though it had completed its important mission. I wasn't ready to go back to the self-loathing of before. I wanted to take pride in every bit of bloated wobble, every stretch mark and every patch of me that had been altered safely delivering my baby into the world.

I was blind to any flaws that might've been visible to others, and filled with the love hormone, oxytocin. Even during the nightmare of the first few weeks I didn't waver on those feelings – but perhaps that's because I was so preoccupied with my painful undercarriage (what a name for it) and battling my way through breastfeeding. I was completely oblivious to the clear change my body had gone through.

Funnily enough, I do remember noticing my body when I went back into hospital with our trio of infections. When I was in a little less discomfort my attention turned to my body when I was getting out of the shower one day. After months of being heavily pregnant I looked at it and felt noticeably slimmer. I said as much when I came out of the bathroom to Tom and Mario, who were sitting there with Buzz. In fact, I'm pretty sure my words were something like, 'Look how flat my tummy's gone already,' while I lifted up my top to show them . . .

It's only now, looking back, that I register the looks on their faces and can read them a little clearer. They smiled kindly at me and nodded in agreement, their foreheads slightly creased as neither really commented. That's because my tummy hadn't gone down. At all. But neither of them had the heart (or possibly the courage) to tell me otherwise. They humoured me. And that is exactly what I needed from them. In that moment I felt good, and that was all that counted.

Those first few weeks after giving birth are so fragile both emotionally and physically, and what others say to you can have a huge effect on your general state of mind. This is something I truly learned after giving birth to Buddy, when someone decided to comment on my I-have-just-pushed-a-baby-out appearance.

Eleven days after I'd given birth we were out of the house and a woman was asking Tom for a picture. She lingered for longer than was comfortable (I was sleep deprived and had just finished feeding a screaming newborn), then she suddenly turned to me, pointed at my tummy and laughed as she said, 'Oh look, Mummy's still got her tummy.'

I was so shocked I laughed.

I laughed because I couldn't quite believe she was pointing out what everyone else had been too kind to draw attention to. I laughed because I couldn't believe a stranger was being so blunt about my jelly belly. I laughed because if I hadn't have done so I'd have cried in her face.

Probably . . .

I remember being really calm and tensing my jaw as she asked me to join in with the photo too. When I declined (I had a baby on my lap, had given birth eleven days before and still had the sorest of foofs) she smiled and said, 'Maybe next time when your face has slimmed down.'

I'll let you digest that for a little bit . . .

Need a bit longer?

Go on then, you have until the next paragraph . . .

The craziest thing is that it was all said with a smile and a giggle, as though we were best mates and I was in on the joke. That's one of the reasons I was so unsure of how to respond. Plus, she'd been going on about her own two children – she was a mother. She'd been through labour, the joys of newborns, and the changes to her own body. Surely that should've made her more aware of what she was saying to me.

I turned to Tom and saw he was just as gobsmacked as I was.

The part of me that really likes to believe in the good of people tells me she didn't mean to offend me. As she was from the Philippines I think it's more likely that there was a little culture clash going on. Perhaps I'm just used to people being politely British and pretending to be oblivious (at least to my face). It's possible she was so giddy about seeing Tom and couldn't believe she was bumping into us so soon after the birth that she got a little overexcited by the whole thing. Or maybe we are simply very different and she's used to interacting with her friends in a different way to me and mine. Who knows. Thankfully, I haven't seen her again to find out.

Whatever the motive behind her words, they played on my mind. Obviously. They also played on Tom's. I know they did because when I next saw his parents they'd already heard about the incident and were telling me how mortified they were.

I did that thing we all do, where I told a couple of other people what had happened in order to gauge their reactions and to check I wasn't being overly sensitive – which with all those hormones flying around was a possibility. I got the same jaw-drop each time, followed by supportive comments and occasionally some expletives. Giorgie was being very protective of me in her usual big sister way, and my mum wanted to go and 'have a word' – I felt like I was back at school and had just told my mum I was being bullied again. Their words and the way they rallied around gave me great comfort.

The words still lingered in my brain for a few days, until one day I got out of the shower and had a good look at my hugely changed body and asked myself how I felt about it. Not just the leftover bump, but the new stretch marks that had formed around my breasts, hips and tummy. The engorged, leaky boobs and the extra weight that sat on my arms, face, thighs and calves . . . The foof that was, like it or not, indefinitely altered. How did I feel about the whole of it? How did I feel about my new body?

The answer?

It was nothing short of a walking miracle.

No hatred.

No nitpicking.

No endless list of flaws I'd love to erase.

Instead a wave of utter gratitude washed over me.

I realised just how grateful I was to my body for working so hard to keep my two little boys safe while they were growing inside me. I was thankful to it for delivering them into the world and showing me the strength I hadn't realised I possessed. I was thankful that my inflated and painful boobs were able to nurse my babies and continue to help them grow and thrive. I was thankful to my leftover bump for showing me, through what it had contained, just how much love I had in my heart, and being the reason I felt an intense surge of unconditional love each and every day. I was thankful to my body for giving me a purpose in life I hadn't known I needed.

My saggy, bruised and swollen body was a marvel, an object of complete beauty in its newly misshapen state.

A newfound peace and self-respect washed over me.

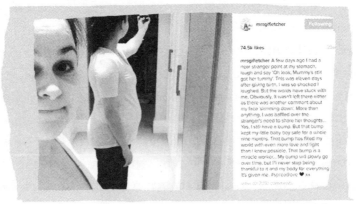

Once I was dressed I decided to take my enlightened attitude to social media, along with a brief account of what had happened with the lady, and a side-on picture of my post-partum tum. The response was astounding. Others started sharing their own stories of the insensitive comments they'd been on the receiving end of, detailing how it had made them feel, how they'd coped and how they'd responded. I couldn't believe how many people had experienced these remarks. With so many women having gone through similar scenarios, it became quite funny. People say inappropriate things from time to time; sadly we were just on the receiving end of these foot-in-mouth moments. It wasn't nice but equally, I wouldn't have wanted to be in Tim from Doncaster's shoes when he asked his daughter's classmate's mum Sharon when the baby was due – only to then notice the face of a grinning four-month-old in the pram next to a perplexed Sharon . . . what a pickle for Tim, who was probably only showing an interest to be polite but had now deeply offended poor Sharon. Sadly, the school pick-up would never be the same again.

But far more importantly than us all realising there's an endless flow of twerps out there who don't think before they speak, the post created a wave of positivity around a topic that can often be crushing for many vulnerable women. I was ecstatic at the number of women who were getting in touch to share their love for their own bodies, my words hitting them with an understanding of how wonderful they actually are, and declaring that we should all be unified by the changes that our bodies go through, and not divided.

That was the point of the post, really: to spread the love I felt, and try not to focus too much on what others might say without thinking. I was lucky enough to be in a good place when the woman said those things to me, but had I been feeling vulnerable, had I been suffering from post-natal depression or simply not coping, I hate to think how her words could've affected me. She'd have completely knocked my confidence at a time when I needed a bit of love. Weeks later, in a moment when I found myself struggling, my mind went back to that comment, and I thanked the heavens it wasn't being made then, because if it had been, I would've completely crumbled.

Hormones are a bitch, but people shouldn't be.

Be kind. Think. And remember you don't *always* have to say what's on your mind.

As a side note to this whole thing, Ashton Kutcher – yes, *the* blooming Ashton Kutcher – shared a link to my post on Facebook, saying, 'These types of comments are not acceptable.'

I totally fangirled!

14

LEARNING THAT SQUIDGY IS THE WAY I AM

LEARNING THAT SQUIDGY IS THE WAY I AM

S adly for me, the Filipino lady's comment wasn't the last time someone made a faux pas regarding my rounded tum. I had a delivery guy, who was so incredibly kind and sweet, tell me not to worry about helping him with the shopping because he could see I was visibly with child (something he did while patting his own tummy to hammer home the point); another man asking if I was getting ready for the new arrival when he found me putting together some white flat-pack furniture; and then, five months after I'd given birth, my gardener asking if I was already pregnant again. To be honest I'd held it together for the previous comments, but my bubble well and truly burst on that one and I had a mammoth, uncontrollable sobbing session.

I had the same reaction when I was due to go on holiday three months after having Buddy and found nothing in my wardrobe fitted me. Literally nothing. I know there have also been times when I've looked in the mirror and given a little deflated sigh at the sight I've been faced with, or simply looked down and felt a sad 'meh', as though I'd given up on my body, or it on me.

Because of what I'd posted online, I felt like I'd become this public figure who was completely accepting of the changes that had occurred to her body. Women were messaging me, telling me they'd read the post and had experienced a change of attitude because of it, and I felt like a fraud. In those moments where I felt the nasty self-critic creep back into the room, I felt like I was letting each of them down. It was a lonely way of thinking, and I shouldn't have put so much pressure on myself. I know that had I shared those thoughts online, I'd have been hit with a wave of understanding comments back, but when you're in it those thoughts can be all-consuming.

What I've realised about these moments is that they're totally normal and fine. A momentary blip of dissatisfaction doesn't mean I'm suddenly ungrateful for everything my body has done for me with my two boys, and will hopefully do again if we decide to add to our brood. It's just me expressing the fact that I'm having a little difficulty adjusting at that particular time. Nor is such a confession vain or superficial. Over the years, just as I did before giving birth, I'm going to experience a wide range of emotions towards my appearance – and that's fine. It doesn't mean I'm failing myself or anyone else. It just means I'm human.

Jeez, us women are complex!

Now, I'm writing this book straight off the back of writing something else, and what with everything going on right now, and the fact that I can't seem to stop eating sugar (I've cut out caffeine so I need something to keep me awake), I know

I'm a good three quarters of a stone heavier than I'd like to be, but I seriously don't have the time to do anything about it right now. It's not an excuse, it's a fact! I have this mental list of priorities, and the physical state of my body is not something I've been able to ponder too heavily. In fact, I barely get a chance to even look at myself in a full-length mirror these days. There always seems to be a child by my side to keep me occupied, or we're in a rush to get somewhere.

It was different when I had just the one, though.

The summer after having Buzz I had two weddings to go to. They became my targets. Before getting pregnant I was nine and a half stone; after giving birth I was twelve and a half. I wanted to drop to ten and a half stone by July, and then ten stone by August. It was a plan formulated in response to my own thoughts and wishes – not carved out for me by someone else's perception of what I should look like.

First things first, three months in, I wanted to fill my body with more goodness. Izzy and Emma had previously talked about Jason Vale's detox juice programmes, so I thought I'd give the five-day one a bash (after checking out it was all fine with breastfeeding, of course). I decided to go for the pre-made, frozen option, to avoid all the faff. Twenty bottles of frozen juice arrived: four bottles each day for five days.

I LOVED IT.

I admit this was incredibly lazy, but part of me just liked knowing that the next meal (juice) was taken care of and that I didn't have to worry about feeding myself – something I never seemed to have time for, so would just grab a quick bite (of sugar) here and there.

In fact, it worked out that each of my juices was timed with Buzz's feeds (ten o'clock, then one, four and seven), so it was quite lovely. We'd both sit there getting our nutrients in and could then get on with the rest of our day afterwards. It was a total time-saver.

My body needed a reboot, like the one I did before I fell pregnant, and although I wasn't eating proper food and was only sipping juice, I loved nothing more than poring over cookbooks once Buzz had gone to bed. I know that sounds absolutely bonkers – why put myself through that torture when I wasn't actually eating anything for five days? – but I was practically salivating over the prospect of the food I was going to eat once I was done. Fresh, organic, good-for-me food. It didn't make me hungry, just really excited. I also got pretty fond of food documentaries on Netflix (I think I've watched all of them) and I started to be more conscious of what I was eating and where it came from. Actually, watching *Earthlings* on YouTube forced Tom and me off meat entirely when the juicing fun was over. Tom became vegan and I a vegetarian. I became obsessed with cookbooks from people like Hemsley and Hemsley, Deliciously Ella and Honestly Healthy. Because I was enjoying what I was doing, it didn't feel like I was depriving myself of anything. If anything, it felt like I was being good to my body, for once.

Unfortunately, when we started getting busier and I went back to work I was less great at cooking us fab vegetable-based meals and instead created the same four meals on a loop. It became boring pretty fast. Plus, when we started weaning Buzz we had to make the decision of whether to give him meat or not. Anyway, I'm veering off-topic now, but just to say our love affair with veganism and vegetarianism lasted a little over six months. Having said that, we still like to be selective about the ingredients we use in our cooking when we can be.

My quest to lose weight wasn't something I was fixated on, but it was something I was aware of. I walked a little more with Buzz (most days started with a walk while he napped) and then watched what I ate after I'd kick-started things with the juicing. It felt nice to have something to aim towards with the weddings. I hit the first target but was a pound over target for the second wedding. I could've got miffed about it and felt deflated and sad, but instead I got off, adjusted the scales slightly (so they favoured my preferred outcome), re-weighed myself and then allowed a feeling of satisfaction at my accomplishment.

Now, I didn't stay there. Over the months that followed I put on a couple of pounds, lost a few and then got stuck at the ten-stone mark again before falling pregnant with Buddy. I haven't seen the underside of ten stone for a few years now. Does that make me feel less of a woman? Does it make me feel unhappy? Does it make me feel unworthy?

If I'm honest, only occasionally.

It usually happens when I have nothing to wear or am wondering when I'm ever going to be able to wear denim hot pants. You see, I've never been able to wear them. My legs have always been the 'rub together at the top' variety, but when I see Abbey Clancy rocking them I feel a silly sadness that I'm never going to be able to do the same. And you know what's utterly ridiculous about that? It's pretty simple. I am never going to have Abbey Clancy's body. I wasn't going to before I had my babies, and I'm pretty sure I'm not going to now, or anytime soon. More importantly, though, I think it's taken me a while to realise that all of us women come in a wide range of sizes and that not one specific size is the 'correct' one. We can't all be size sixes, because most of us just aren't born that way. We are all unique, and that individuality is what makes us all beautiful.

It's been a long road, but I've finally come to terms with the fact that beauty doesn't come from being able to fit into a pair of size six hot pants, but rather from a grounded contentment with what you're rocking in the body department. My failure when it comes to hot pants doesn't make me a lesser human being – although I do feel sorry for the hot pants that they'll never know the feel of my squidgy sides being pressed against their unforgiving fabric. Ha!

I know there'll be moments when I wobble, times when I emotionally crumble because my tummy seems bigger than I find acceptable or my bingo wings shake with more ferocity than normal and catch my attention. And that's fine. It's fine for me to go through those feelings. It's fine for me to then empower myself by doing something about it and starting a new workout routine because I want to feel healthier or even slimmer. It's fine because it will have come from me and my own desires for my body, not someone else's ideals for it. It's fine because I am a woman and I understand my body weight fluctuates on a monthly basis. It's fine because I understand the reasons for that. It's fine because ultimately I love my body and am in awe of all it has given me.

It. Is. All. Fine.

15

SO MANY CLASSES, SO LITTLE TIME!

SO MANY CLASSES, SO LITTLE TIME!

When Buzz was ten weeks old I suddenly felt like I should be doing more with him. Talking to him or putting him on his jungle mat was no longer enough. I needed to be stimulating him, making the most of his sponge-like brain, fuelling his (newly) inquisitive mind and ensuring he had a bright future ahead of him. Basically Tom had read an article in the *National Geographic* about a child's brain and how new things trigger neurons to open up, send signals, or be released . . . or something like that, I can't really remember. But the general gist of what I understood it to mean was that the more interaction babies got, the more unlocked their brains became (sorry to any scientists who might be reading this book and are sitting aghast at my appalling explanation – it's like a medical game of Chinese Whispers, and as we all know that game never ends well).

In my bid to be 'the best mum ever' and unlock my child's

brain, I searched around for some local classes I could do with him. There was so much to choose from, it was almost impossible to pick. I ended up opting for four. The first one was a follow-on from a pregnancy yoga class I'd done before Buzz arrived, only this time the sessions were baby focused with a little baby yoga, reflexology and massage. Next we had swimming – something I was very passionate about him doing because I had hearing difficulties as a child, which resulted in me not being the world's strongest swimmer thanks to me not being allowed to dunk my head under water. More than that, though, I wanted Buzz to feel happy and confident in the water and on holiday I'd seen a little twenty-month-old girl who was swimming like a fish. Such a contrast to the fear I used to feel.

The next class was baby sensory, where we'd sing different songs and shake a plethora of shiny, glittery objects in their faces to aid their development. And finally there was Tiny Talk – baby signing.

I'd gone from having no real structure to our week to having an extremely busy baby-class-led one. I hadn't properly thought through what sort of an impact that would have on our days, but needless to say it was a dramatic one.

Walking into a room full of women can be daunting at the best of times (I'm initially rubbish in big gatherings, something that goes back to being bullied in school and has left me feeling paranoid that people – groups of women in particular – are looking at me and judging), and it can be even tougher when walking in with a newborn. Pre-baby, a scenario like that would have had me feeling like all of my flaws had been amplified and exposed, but adding a baby into the mix made my skin crawl with anxiety. Everyone always seemed so much better at the mum game that I was. I would suddenly worry that Buzz was dressed inadequately and fret that I should've put on his extra-thick cardi as well as the millions of other layers he was wearing. Mostly I'd worry about what Buzz might do in that forty-five-minute session. He was in his crying phase (still) when we joined all of these classes, and he was prone to the odd meltdown. He'd usually be angelic and engaged up to a certain point, and would then cry and cry. Back then I didn't feed in public. I just couldn't do it, so I'd always introduce a cheeky extra feed before classes began, so I'd know he wasn't hungry. If he started crying I'd check his nappy, give him a cuddle, see if it was wind . . . When nothing worked eventually I'd reach for the emergency dummy, feeling like a completely useless mummy as I unleashed it from its little box and guided it into Buzz's wailing mouth. He'd stop instantly, and then fall asleep, while I'd stand there with a case of the mum sweats, feeling exposed for my failure. Clearly experiences like that affected my enjoyment of these classes, which is a huge shame because one of their main aims is not just to grow your child's skill set (I know they're only months old but remember that brain-unlocking thingy), but to have some lovely mummy and baby bonding time. I did not feel like I experienced that in the majority of classes I attended in those early days – and that's not the fault of the classes or the teachers, but to do with my own ridiculousness. I'd spend the whole class praying Buzz didn't cry and would then get a complete sweat on when he did. It felt like I flapped a lot, but really I think I was back to doing my best duck impression again, and giving off lots of super calm mum zen.

At that point in time it was all just a bit too much. I had

something organised for almost every weekday, but it left me feeling like there was no room for being spontaneous because it was still a military operation to get us out of the house with everything we needed. It felt so stifling to have so many plans. Plus a few of the classes overlapped with the sleep plan I was trying to enforce – I mean, not that Buzz would've let himself have that nap anyway, but it was impossible to even try and stick to any sort of routine when there was so much external stuff going on. Blah, blah, blah . . . the long and the short of it is that I just took on too much too soon, so I dropped two of the classes and ended up just going to baby signing and swimming.

We all loved, and continue to love, baby sign (but now with Buddy instead). It was a class I'd stumbled upon by accident, thinking it said 'singing' on the website and not 'signing'. My mum brain had clearly affected my reading skills, but I'm glad it did as singing is still a huge part of the class and the new communication tool of signing has been INVALUABLE to us as a family. Honestly, I wasn't sure at first – babies using their hands to communicate even though they couldn't talk seemed highly unlikely to me. But the teacher, Louisa, is such an energetic and bubbly lady, we found ourselves enjoying the class regardless. Both boys have been utterly captivated in class from the start – and that's all Louisa's doing. We'd learn a few signs in class while singing songs, and then it would be up to us parents to use them at home. See it, say it, sign it, is always Louisa's motto, and that's what we did.

I felt like a plonker when I first started doing them – focusing purely on milk to begin with. Every time I was about to feed Buzz I'd do the sign. One day he just got really excited by it, so I knew he understood. It wasn't long until he started doing the sign himself, telling us that he wanted milk, or that he understood it was time for milk. He'd go for it with great gusto, bouncing up and down in his seat as he did it. This was something all of our friends and family found fascinating – especially Dougie, Tom's McFly bandmate, who found it funny that the sign was linked to my boobs. He'd do the sign to Buzz, but then would have to apologise when it wasn't time for a feed and Buzz got disappointed (something a little distraction would help to ease).

After Buzz had managed milk, he mastered other signs fairly quickly. By the time he was one year old he could sign food, nappy, duck, more, all gone, and he was also clapping, waving and asking to be picked up. Only a couple of months later and he was up to over twenty signs including helicopter, plane, tree, boat, wash, bath . . . it was amazing and very handy. Buzz loved the fact we understood him when he wanted more food or was thirsty – you could see the joy ping onto his face when he realised we knew what he was telling us.

He stopped going to class when Louisa went on maternity leave, but really he'd started to say more by that point so the signs weren't as necessary anyway. He now has an obsession with Mr Tumble, who I really wasn't sure about at first, but you can't choose your child's idols and we now love him too. Buzz has a little spotty bag like Mr Tumble, in which he carries his 'tumble tap' (a Fisher Price ABC tablet). He plonks himself down next to us and says lines like, 'Let's look inside Mr Tumble's spotty bag and see what he wants us to look for today.' It's incredibly cute, and wondrous to see his language developing.

We've now started taking Buddy to baby sign and he seems to be enjoying it just as much as Buzz did. Tom thought he signed 'all gone' after dinner the other night, but I wasn't so sure – the milk sign is definitely getting a reaction, though.

• • • • •

Despite my earlier fears and my own set of judgments, most of the other mums in the classes I attended were lovely, especially in baby signing. I was wrong to think anyone had been judging me and therefore I felt bad that I had been judging them for judging me. Ha! I think in that situation most mums are just concerned with themselves and whatever their own baby's doing, or maybe thinking about the millions of other things going on in their lives.

In any case, I soon realised that baby groups are a serious source of support for what is indisputably the craziest time of your life. Being in a room with other mums instantly means you can share! Sharing is great. Sharing is your friend. It's only when you start talking that you begin to realise you aren't alone in your thinking and your struggles. In many ways baby groups are like a speed-dating event. At some point you'll sit next to another mum who you really click with, and then you'll sit together each week. It's quite lovely. I've met a few mums in this way and we've since become what I'll fondly refer to as 'Whatsapp support'. We don't get to meet up because of our schedules, but we're always there at the end of our phones when needed, or to just check in every now and then. Seeing as I never did any NCT classes it's really nice to feel like I have some local friends with children. We might have lived in our house for almost eleven years now, but we moved here with all the McFly boys (not into the same house, but we could see into their living rooms and our front door was always unlocked for them to be able to waltz in at any moment) and never really ventured out of our friendship circle or beyond our lovely neighbours (Hi Jacqui and Pete!). Although we're perfectly happy with our own company or travelling to see friends and family, it's lovely to finally feel part of a community somehow, especially now that all the other McFly guys have moved away.

Obviously, not all mums became ladies I could rely on or wanted to befriend, and it didn't take me long to realise the sort of person who might rub me up the wrong way – i.e. anyone who's so forceful with their opinion that they criticise others. One mum came in a little tense to one of the morning classes because she'd been having a debate online about breastfeeding. She was still looking at her phone, steam shooting from her ears. I could feel her judgment and negativity seeping into my newly anxious soul and it made me feel really uncomfortable. The same mum would wade in with her opinion during chats and shoot down others if their views differed from her own. It was pretty full on.

The thing is, I don't blame her for wanting to use the time with other parents to express herself (babies give you no chatter back), and really I've no idea what her situation was or whether she was coping or not, but I think I prefer to be more accepting of others and liked chatting to mums who were a little more laid-back and open in their approach.

Scrap all that, she just intimidated me, and at a time when I needed a little more love and encouragement, I found it tough to deal with. It felt good to bond over a shared lack of sleep, rather than try and batter each other with our opinions . . . Luckily there was no one like that in either swimming (which has never really been a class you can socialise in) or baby signing, and now that I'm a more experienced mum I've learned to close myself off to others who make me question myself – two happy babies in, I must be doing something right!

Tom ended up taking Buzz and now Buddy to the majority of his swimming and baby sign lessons. He got used to being the only dad in the room pretty quickly (although he's seen more and more dads join him along the way) and seems to really relish that one-on-one time with the boys. I would love to still be going along, but I've had to get back to work – which largely means sitting in my office all day long and staring at my computer while hearing Tom and the boys playing in the other room – although his schedule is just as busy as mine right now.

It's a funny thing, writing – people know you're at home while your child is being taken care of by someone else and I'm sure they imagine you're sitting around watching daytime TV while scooping up mounds of Nutella, but I can confirm that only part of that sentence is true. Ha!

16
GETTING BACK TO WORK

GETTING BACK TO WORK

I knew before Buzz was born that I'd have to start writing again when he was around six months old. That way I could stick to my publishing schedule, which was something I was really keen to do as I'd only had two novels published by that point. It felt like a premature time in my author career to have a huge gap between publications and I didn't want what I'd already achieved to just fade into nothing. I knew that if I wanted to fully establish myself in the literary world then I had to keep going and not have longer than a year between books. I'd planned with my fabulous editor to hand in the first draft of my third novel, *Dream a Little Dream*, a year after Buzz was born. That gave me six months' maternity leave, and six months to write the book. I knew it was going to be a tight turnaround, but I was familiar with my method of writing and knew I was up to the challenge. I also repeatedly told myself how lucky I was that I'd be able to work from home and that I'd still see Buzz all day – I know some mums have to be out of the house for the majority of the working day, so it seemed I had the perfect job to work alongside motherhood. I'd been told through a friend that one author used to have her child peacefully asleep next to her while she cracked on with her writing (and she writes extraordinary books), so I had a wonderful vision of my baby in his bouncer, gurgling away, while I did the same – elegantly using my toe to rock his chair every so often.

Hahahahahaaaa . . . fool!

It became clear to me that this fantasy scenario I'd dreamed up simply wasn't for us. Buzz needed more from his daytime companion. He lived off 90-minute naps and needed stimulation. I knew I wouldn't be able to give him that and work at the same time.

Having the end of my maternity leave looming in the distance was difficult, as I expect it is for most mums. The realisation that I wasn't going to be spending every second of the day with the little human I'd been spending every second of the day with since he'd arrived was incredibly tough. Whenever I thought about it I'd experience this heaviness in my heart – as though I was already starting to miss him even though he was still *with* me. This feeling intensified the closer I got to the change occurring, but even more so at the five-month mark, because it was at this point that Buzz's personality seemed to switch on. He became a completely different baby. He was super funny and interactive. He suddenly stopped crying and decided to laugh at everything instead (something that, rather interestingly, Buddy also did at around this point). And he really loved me – this was just so very clear. He would love snuggling into me, burying himself in my arms. Searching for me in a room and crying if I left, his sweet little face absolutely lighting up just at the sight of me returning. I'd never felt so loved, needed and whole. How could I possibly turn my back on that? On him!

Well, the reality is that in order to work, I had to. A part of me also wanted a piece of normality back – something that's difficult to admit as a mum. It's hard to say you miss having no feed and nap schedule to adhere to, an unbroken adult conversation, or a time where you were allowed to have a bit of time to yourself without being made to feel guilty for it. Having a baby robs you of that (in a lovely way, of course), leaving you to feel that the only alone time you have is when you're on the toilet – and you're not always even granted that luxury. I can remember in the early days actually holding Buzz while I went to the loo because he kept screaming any time I put him down. There didn't seem to be a happy alternative in that moment so I just went with it. It was a scenario that happened more than once – which was hardly surprising with my wailer of a newborn. Luckily I've now perfected the one-armed loo visit.

There were occasions when the prospect of sitting down at my desk and getting 'back in the zone' filled me with excitement. It wasn't a slog to get back to work, but it certainly churned up a whole heap of complex emotions within me. Just admitting to myself that I was looking forward to it made me feel like a terrible and undeserving mum. And it's not that Buzz had done anything wrong, it's not that I didn't want to be with him or wasn't grateful for him . . . It's just that I had a career to be getting back to. Gosh, just writing that down seems so selfish!

Funnily enough, growing up, I always pictured myself being a stay-at-home mum. That was my role, that was my calling.

That was where I knew I'd be most content. I don't think the opposite is true, but I suddenly found myself in the position of having a successful career ahead of me, and fancied my luck at trying both. And I do think that's a generational difference. Back in my mum's day you were usually one or the other – a mother, or a career woman. Nowadays I think we are given the opportunity to be both if we want to be. And, for the record, I think either choice is perfectly fine. I don't think women should be made to feel guilty or selfish for going back to work, but equally I don't think women should be made to feel less worthy or unambitious if they stay at home. We are all different. We all have different things going on behind those closed doors of ours. Just like breastfeeding, it's for the individual mother and family to work out what's best for their situation, and not waste their time seeking the approval of others who aren't in their shoes. Having said that, it was my own past visions of my future life as a mum that made me feel incredibly guilty for spending some of my time away from my important role as a mother. But mother's guilt is something I think I will battle with forever more!

It was tough organising what we were going to do with Buzz while I was working (Tom was recording an album with the McBusted boys by that point, with McFly on a little hiatus while the bands joined forces), but in the end we decided to recruit Tom's mum. That way we could be flexible with hours (both our jobs can be unpredictable) and we'd feel safer knowing he was with his nanna, and comforted by the fact he was still going to be with family and feel loved.

Although I was happy with the decision we'd come to, I still found myself incredibly upset. In fact, the day Debbie handed in her notice at work and our plans were confirmed,

I sobbed. I didn't want anyone else to be looking after my baby. *I* should've been looking after him . . . Obviously I could've changed my writing plans – I know my editor would've been more than supportive if I'd have said I was unhappy – but I was aware it wasn't something I wanted to do. Instead we asked Debbie to come over to ours two to three days a week at first, so that she could have him there while I worked in the office. That way I could take him off for a feed and then have lunch with him too. It worked well for a while, and helped both Buzz and me get used to not being together every second of the day, but I probably wasn't being the most productive I've ever been. Also, as I'm sure you're aware if you've ever been around one, babies are noisy! Whenever I heard him I wanted to go and see him and find out what he was up to. Likewise, if I wanted a drink or to go to the loo, I'd get pulled from my world of writing and sucked into theirs, my heart aching to play. I was easily distracted.

It was soon decided that Buzz would go to his nanna and ewad's house on the days I was working from home. Firstly, Debbie understandably felt more comfortable there, and secondly it would give me a peaceful house to write in. It was something I dug my heels in over for a while – I didn't want to admit that I couldn't have him at home with me – BUT the ironic thing is that the more focused days of writing I am blessed with, the fewer of them I actually need.

I felt incredibly lonely the first day Buzz wasn't in the house with me, but my reward was a good chunky word count at the end of the six hours and a very smiley baby who was thrilled to be reunited with me.

It wasn't plain sailing, of course. There were days I'd sit at my desk, staring at a blank screen, and a picture would ping up of Buzz from whichever family member had him that day (sometimes my dad, mum, or Mario would come over for some one-to-one time with him). Buzz on a swing, loving life. Buzz in the seat of a trolley, loving life. I wasn't there the first time he did either of those things. I cried when both of those pictures came through, asking myself what the buggery I thought I was doing away from my baby when it was my role to bring him up. Instead I was at my desk, closed off from the world around me as I tried to immerse myself in the life of my characters. I don't think it's a coincidence that the bunch of friends created in *Dream a Little Dream* have been my favourite fictional friends to date. They were such a supportive bunch – they were exactly what I needed at that point in time.

• • • • •

With Buddy I planned a full year of maternity leave. I wanted time away to focus on my family, and fully realise my potential as a mum. That was my plan. I was adamant that my editor wouldn't charm me into anything else . . . and then I got blooming inspired and creative. Before I gave birth I ended up going to the publishers with an original idea that they loved, so I knew I'd be working on that as soon as I felt ready.

Timing was everything. I needed to get ready to juggle those balls and spin those plates. Little did I know I'd be juggling and spinning a mere three days into life with two little ones to run around after, as my copy-edit for my fourth novel, *Always With Love*, had arrived back.

I could've left it for a couple of weeks and then gone back to it, but with Tom at home more there was less of a fog surrounding those first few weeks of having a newborn. So I puffed up my ring cushion (usually meant for when you've got piles, but it totally helped me and my tender 'down below'), sat at my desk and got to work while Buddy slept in his Moses basket. To be fair, it was only one solid day of work, but still – I was back at it nonetheless. Six weeks later my creative juices were flowing and I decided to get cracking on my new secret project. I wasn't even halfway through that book before coming up with the concept for this one.

It's mind-boggling to me how I went from wanting a year off to writing three books in a year. What a blooming nutter.

17

CHILDREN SHOULD BE
BANNED FROM FLYING

CHILDREN SHOULD BE BANNED FROM FLYING

My dad is an extremely laid-back man; however, there is one area in life he's pretty enthusiastic and vocal about, and that's anything concerning my nonna. Even before Buzz was born he was asking me about getting a passport so that Nonna (who is too old to comfortably travel over to England now) could meet the new arrival. It was something that he brought up in conversation literally every single time we spoke – he wanted to know when I was thinking of going over and he suggested we look into flights. It was incredibly sweet that he was so eager for his mum to meet his first grandchild.

So when Buzz was a few weeks old we took him to a photo booth and tried to get a decent snap of him . . . we failed miserably, mainly because there are so many rules about passport photos and what you can and can't have/do in the picture. We tried to do it with Tom's arm holding Buzz up, so that his arm was out of shot. The method worked in terms of keeping Tom unseen, but Buzz just seemed to curl up, his knees wanting to be up in his chest. We couldn't get his face in the big oval shape on the computer screen without including the rest of his body – not without upsetting him, anyway. The photos we took were hilarious as his curled-up position gave him the world's biggest double chin and made him look incredibly grumpy. He was pulling the strangest of faces and the photos taken looked nothing like him at all – which I know is a silly thought when talking about a baby who's only a few weeks old, but I felt the picture should bear *some* resemblance to the passport holder.

We tried once more but it just wasn't working, so we ended up jumping into the booth with him and having some funny shots taken of all three of us instead.

It wasn't until after this failure that I heard about a few online companies that take existing photos and make them passport-control compatible. I was pretty chuffed with the discovery as it meant I could use one of my favourite pictures of him. So, in spite of the kerfuffle at the booth, he actually ended up with a rather nice photo in the end.

Once the perfect passport picture was obtained we then had to go into town to get Buzz's passport. I'm not entirely sure why I did this trip with a newborn when I could've just done the whole thing by post and saved myself the hassle, but that's the plan my baby brain hatched. It was a pretty uneventful trip (minus one of Buzz's usual mini-meltdowns) and before long we had his first ever passport. It's crazy to think that he'll have that particular one until he's five years old though, as despite my best efforts it already looks nothing like him!

With the passport in hand we could finally book the trip to Italy. Dad was going to be over there for two weeks that

August, but I didn't fancy going for that long with a five-month-old baby, so decided to opt for a long weekend instead. Sadly Tom couldn't make it because he was working, meaning it would be just my dad and me for the first couple of days before Mario flew over to join us for my dad's birthday. That also meant I had someone to fly back with – which was something I was grateful for as the thought of getting on a flight on my own with Buzz was giving me a return of the mum sweats (they bizarrely left once I stopped wearing my nursing pads, along with the smell I seemed to create even when clean – turns out my baps just needed airing).

While looking into flights I did something I never normally do: I cheekily emailed an airline's PR, saying I was going to document the trip for my *Hello!* blog as it was my first flight with Buzz, in the hope that she might help me out in some way. Yeah, it didn't work. The lady basically emailed back a link to the online booking site with a polite message about the airline's great two-piece extra baggage allowance for infants (for prams, car seats or travel cots) and wished me a safe flight. I'm not sure exactly what I was expecting; I think I was just having a mild panic at the thought of travelling with a baby. To be fair, though, the contact did help when Dad and I realised we'd be sitting separately because we hadn't booked in one party or chosen our seats – she was really helpful then and made sure we were together.

My anxiety over the flight wasn't helped when I turned on *This Morning* one day and found myself watching a debate on whether children should even be *allowed* on flights. The woman arguing against their presence (despite having a ten-year-old of her own) was being quite judgmental towards other parents, and insulting, rude and outlandish in her remarks to hosts Ruth and Eamonn. Now, I know how TV works. Producers like a good debate to get under the skin of viewers so that they feel compelled to get involved and engaged, but even though I knew that was the case, I still felt defensive for every parent who has ever had to get on a flight with a child before. I felt my insides shrivel as my anxiety grew.

I got myself worked up, going so far as to pick up my phone and hammer out a great response on Twitter. I chickened out and deleted the post before pressing the send button, deciding to remove myself from my spot in front of the TV instead. Getting involved with debates like that is just not good for my health. But although I had removed myself from the debate, the conversation stayed with me. When high up in the sky, contained in a small flying vessel, was I going to feel as though everyone was against me because I'd turned up with a baby? What if he cried the whole time? What if someone said something to me, or showed their abhorrence at Buzz's presence?

Well, you can't really plan when travelling with a child. I basically got majorly paranoid that I was going to be heckled off the flight and shamed by the other passengers as soon as they saw me getting on the plane with my arms loaded – after all, if that angry lady on *This Morning* was anything to go by, they would all hate the very sight of me and my un-flight-worthy baby. I was thankful I was going to have my dad or brother there for moral support.

Aside from the social politics of the whole thing, I was particularly worried about Buzz's ears on the flight, as I'd suffered so horrifically with bad ears as a child. Even in my teens I can remember being in tears at the pressure my sensitive ears used to feel on take-off and landing, so I wanted to make sure I did as much as I could to prevent that. Turns out

I had the perfect soother on my person already – boobs! Feeding when we took off and then again when we started to descend was the best tip I ever received concerning babies and flying.

· · · · ·

Funnily enough this trip produced the footage for my first ever YouTube video. Tom had been trying to get me to start vlogging for a while, but I just didn't see what the fuss was about. I clearly hadn't watched anyone else online, because once I did I was hooked and thought I'd start playing around with it. Basically I just filmed everything I found interesting, deciding to work out how to make it into something when I got back.

Spoiler alert: I loved the finished product, plus it's given me a lovely little keepsake of the trip, which is undoubtedly a huge advantage of compiling all the videos I have made in the last two and a half years.

The footage shows my dad and I meeting at the airport, and then giddily smiling at the camera during take-off while Buzz was asleep in my arms. We'd booked a ridiculously early flight, around 6 a.m., meaning Buzz hadn't had a full night's sleep before I took him from his cot and popped him in a car seat. He was shattered when we got to our seats and conked out straight after I fed him – which I think was before the plane had even moved from its stationary spot on the tarmac.

I had hardly slept the night before because I was worried about what the flight would entail, my mind going through each scenario and how I'd react to any adverse comments (smile – always smile). I needn't have worried. Buzz slept most of the way, waking up in time for a feed before we got there. He seemed unaffected by the change of altitude. It was a huge success – I arrived feeling knackered, frazzled and hugely relieved!

And it was completely worth the stress (even if it was only created by my own mind going into overdrive) as the sight of my nonna playing with Buzz and making him chuckle was a mammoth delight. The whole trip was lovely – but then what's not to love about having a few days focused around food, drink and sleep while having some quality time with my son, dad, nonna and, eventually, brother?

There's something so warming about going back to Valva with Dad. Even though he left for England when he was nineteen, everyone in the village still knows who he is and welcomes him with gusto and enthusiasm. There's a real sense of togetherness within the community, with people continuously stopping in to drop off eggs, nuts or vegetables they've grown on their farms. It's comforting to know this also happens when we aren't there, and that people are still going in to see my nonna with treats. As she's got older, work on her own garden has stopped, but instead of trading eggs for something like fresh homegrown potatoes, tomatoes or figs, she offers a slab of chocolate that Dad has brought her from England. As far as I know, no one's complained just yet.

· · · · ·

Since that trip Nonna has met Buddy, too. As predicted, Dad was keen for us to book in the trip at the first opportunity we could, so we went when he was a few months old. This time we all went, with Tom, Giorgie, Mario, Chickpea and Debbie coming along too. It was far busier (we needed to hire a minibus) but it was nice to all be away together with no real plan or forced structure to our days. We could just relax and enjoy each other's company – something that seems far easier to do when we're completely away from our homes and have terrible phone reception while up in the mountains.

This time Buzz could fully appreciate seeing Nonna. I loved hearing him call her 'Great Nooona' and being affectionate towards her. And the fondness went both ways, with Nonna being particularly happy that Buzz has a great appetite and was open to trying anything she offered him (he was probably too scared to do otherwise). She didn't even mind when he stole her zimmer frame and walked up and down the driveway with it as though it was a car. I hope this bond will have years to grow and flourish, and I'm so happy the boys have been able to meet the absolute matriarch of our family.

• • • • •

I've just mentioned to my dad that I'm writing this chapter. He responded by telling me we have to look into flights for our next trip, so that we can introduce the newest member of the family, my sister's girl Summer Rae, to Nonna, too. Ha! I imagine this will be discussed in every conversation we have until it's booked. Not that I mind. I'm looking forward to going over to Valva a lot in the coming years as our family grows bigger and bigger.

18

BOOBS OUT ON THE EUROSTAR

BOOBS OUT ON THE EUROSTAR

Before we headed over to Italy to see my nonna, we were invited to Disneyland Paris to celebrate the fact that Tom had won Celebrity Dad of the Year 2014, and the opening of their new 'Ratatouille' ride. Now, we'd always said that we wouldn't take Buzz over to one of the Disney parks until he was old enough to really soak up the magic, but when you're invited to go to one by some nice PR folk, it's impossible to say no. Especially as Tom was going to be over in Paris that weekend anyway as McBusted were supporting One Direction on some of their world tour dates. We decided to take them up on the offer, with Buzz and me meeting Tom over there.

Obviously Buzz wasn't going to be captivated or possibly even engaged by his surroundings, but it's Disney. And one thing you should know about us Fletchers is that we love all things Disney! (Emma once made the observation that there's not a single room in our house that doesn't have something Mickey or Minnie-related in it.)

It seemed the easiest way of getting over to Paris was on the Eurostar. As it was only for two nights and Tom was going over there before we were I sent him off with our stuff so that I'd only be left with a small bag of travel essentials (it's never a *small* bag, it's always the entire contents of Buzz's room, JUST IN CASE), a car seat on my Bugaboo base, and, most importantly, Buzz.

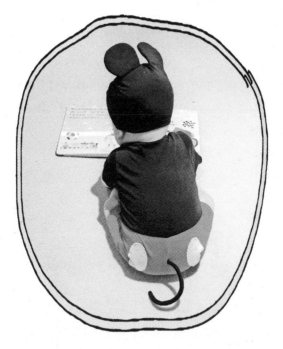

I felt wonderfully in control as I arrived at King's Cross St Pancras station with plenty of time to spare. Sleeping Buzz and I breezed through security (the staff were exceptionally friendly to the lady travelling with a baby), and I even treated myself to a bacon butty (and a chocolate caramel slice – must remember this book is all about honesty) while I flicked leisurely through a glossy magazine as we waited to board our train.

I was travelling with a baby, and I know I looked like I had that shizzle down. All my organising had paid off and I was set to breeze through the whole thing.

Go me!

I got on the train and was delighted to see that my seat was at a table in a group of four, and that the carriage was fairly quiet. There were a few people dotted around the place and a family of four to my left, but the children were both teenagers and engrossed in their iPads, so I knew they were going to be keeping themselves to themselves for the trip. It was going to be a nice chilled-out couple of hours, I told myself.

I popped Buzz's car seat in the chair next to me and we snuggled in for the ride, with me feeling like a total mum boss.

As I still wasn't feeling the desire to breastfeed in public, I had decided to take some bottled expressed milk with me for the journey, along with a flask of boiling water and plastic cup, so I could heat it up at a moment's notice without having to rely on anyone else to help.

I thought I was being clever and prepared.

Buzz thought I was being a jerk.

He was confused as to why I was giving him milk from a bottle when I could give it to him from source. While he pulled that bemused expression, it dawned on me that, as he was going to sleep at 7 p.m. and had cut out his 10 p.m. feed altogether, we'd stopped giving him the expressed bottle feed in the evenings. We hadn't even thought about moving that bottle feed earlier so that he still had the bottle in his life . . . He'd not had a bottle for a few weeks when we stepped on the train. And he wasn't happy to see it return.

He wailed because he was hungry, but then turned his head away from the bottle, as though turning his nose up at it – while continuing to cry. At one point he even blew a disgusted raspberry at the mumma juice hiding behind the plastic teat, meaning I got a face full of the stuff.

Lovely.

I no longer looked like a mumma that had her shizzle together. I was a sweaty mumma with breast milk dotted all over her face.

Epic fail.

Buzz was having a full-on meltdown and I was having a full-on flapping session as I tried my best to appease him and encourage him to take the flipping bottle while trying to look calm.

I figured I had two options: either let him wail and feel like a terrible mother while other passengers looked on aghast, or save all of our ears and actually feed him from my human jugs. Unsurprisingly, I decided on the second option.

I was completely covered up as I had a scarf on and everything, but I still couldn't look anyone in the eye as I fed Buzz. I could feel the eyes of the teenagers as they lost interest in their screens and started looking over. Not only that, but our nice quiet carriage suddenly became as busy as the A40 on a Monday morning, with streams of people on the hunt for the toilet or the buffet cart. The carriage was full of activity now that I had a boob on the loose.

I might've wanted the ground to swallow me up, but my child was content and no longer wailing like a banshee. I guess we were all winners really.

Sadly Buzz didn't go back on the bottle without a fight. It took a lot of perseverance from Tom to get him accepting it again. It was horrible, but something we had to go through if we ever wanted anyone else to look after him while I worked. Needless to say, when he finally succumbed to our will we made sure we kept the seven o'clock bedtime feed as a bottle one! The experience has also kept us on our toes with Buddy and we make sure he doesn't go more than a few days without having a feed from a bottle.

With Buzz fed, a sense of calm was reinstated to our trip. I loved Disneyland Paris. Yes, Buzz was too young to enjoy it properly, but it felt good to have a glimpse of the magic for ourselves and imagine what it was going to be like when we went back with him in the future, when he could really be swept away by the wonder of it all.

We broke our no-Disney rule a second time, actually. We went to LA when Buzz was only fourteen months old and spent five days of our three weeks over there in Anaheim, at Disneyland.

But instead of telling you about that, perhaps I should tell you about our trip to Australia, and how I travelled twenty-four hours with an eleven-month-old . . .

19

AN ADVENTURE DOWN UNDER

(NO, THIS ISN'T A CHAPTER ABOUT MY NUNNY OR OUR SEX LIFE)

AN ADVENTURE DOWN UNDER

(NO, THIS ISN'T A CHAPTER ABOUT MY NUNNY OR OUR SEX LIFE)

W hen Tom told me the One Direction tour was going to take them to Australia for three weeks, I knew there was no way Buzz and I were going to stay at home. Not a chance. It was far too long to be apart, for a start, but then there was also the fact that I absolutely love Oz and would have been a miserable cow if I'd been left behind!

I'd stayed in Sydney while the McFly boys were over there recording their album *Motion in the Ocean* back in 2008, and I absolutely fell in love with the place – the people are friendly and welcoming, the place is gorgeous and the weather is far warmer than here. If it hadn't been for the fact my friends, family and all my work commitments were back in the UK I'd have become an expat in a second. So I was thrilled at the prospect of going back and having a bit of a break from gloomy London.

I did have the small matter of continuing to write a book while I was out there, and a baby to keep occupied, but I was sure I could keep juggling and make the most of having fun daytime adventures with Buzz and then having focused time on my laptop in the evenings when he was asleep. I got so excited at the thought of being over there with him and being able to enjoy a slower pace of life together.

As the trip was part of an Australian tour, it meant there were quite a few stops along the way – Sydney, Melbourne, Adelaide, Perth and Brisbane. I felt it was going to be a bit too much to do all that flying with Buzz (as some of the stopovers were only for two or three nights before getting on another flight to the next location), so I decided to cut out Brisbane and Perth. That way I'd still feel we were a part of the trip, but we'd be more settled by staying in one place a little longer. Sydney was set to be our main base, which was something I was ecstatic about as I knew it a tad better than the other places and would therefore feel more comfortable there alone while the group travelled on without us.

It took me weeks to pack our cases. I kept building piles of necessities in the spare room – the mountain of much-needed belongings becoming bigger and bigger. Let's make something clear from the start – they were all things for Buzz. Three weeks away from home basically required me to pack everything we owned for him, and he also had to get a brand-new wardrobe especially for the trip (lucky little thing!) as it was going to be summer over there and he had outgrown all his cooler clothes from our summer, which had ended several months before.

One thing I've learned since becoming a mum is that I don't actually need any of my own possessions in our hand luggage, or even in our day-to-day changing bag. I need nothing that isn't baby-related. It's just extra weight to carry around and struggle with. Long gone are the days where I'd carry a book in my bag, a magazine or even a bit of make-up to touch up my face if I felt the need to freshen up. As there is no longer any time to freshen up or do a little light reading, these luxuries have become redundant. An extra nappy or toy in the bag would be much more useful than something I wouldn't even take out.

And that was what it was like flying to Oz, with Buzz managing to hog most of the space in our two suitcases with his endless paraphernalia. I took everything I could think of, even nappies. Of course, I realised that they did sell nappies in Australia, as well as all of the snacks Buzz liked to eat, and the toys he liked to play with, or the books he liked to read, but I didn't feel the need to make life simpler for myself when travelling with a ten-month-old baby. Nope. Out came my jeans, the fancy dress I probably wouldn't wear and the spare flip-flops, and in went the Ella's Kitchen pouches, Little Dish nibbles and a fab selection of Peppa Pig books. A happy and contented baby who didn't feel like his world had changed dramatically overnight was what I was after. It was worth sacrificing my summer wardrobe for . . . it wasn't like any of it fitted, anyway.

Now we just had to endure the flight.

Tom and the McBusted guys were heading to Japan before Oz for some promo, meaning I was going to have to do the twenty-four-hour flight without him. Izzy and Georgia were there too (we were all making the most of the McBusted excursion down under), so I wasn't completely alone. However, travelling with friends is never the same as travelling with someone who carries the same weight of responsibility as you do – no matter how willing they are to step in and help.

Even though I'd been on a flight with Buzz before, I knew a long-haul one was a completely different ball game. It was a long time to keep Buzz happy and entertained for, and I knew there were going to be meltdowns from both of us along the way. It wasn't a negative way of looking at things, I generally like to look for the good in any situation, but it was practical and realistic and got me ready for what lay ahead (though it did also make me extremely tense and anxious).

To get myself prepared I searched the internet for wise words, swotting up for the occasion in the hope that someone would enlighten me about what to expect. I went to vlogs and blogs, loving the personal accounts from fellow parents as they imparted their wisdom, but I also scoured books, articles and airline websites for clues on how to make the whole experience as pleasant as possible. I found the words from one Australian airline a total comfort when reading a paragraph on why children might cry on planes:

'It is not uncommon for an infant to cry, and/or put their hands over their ears, during take-off and landing. Please do not be alarmed or feel embarrassed. Crying is a natural way for your infant to clear their ears – it is best to let them go.'

It was such a friendly approach to the whole thing and vastly different from the snotty attitudes I'd been expecting from anyone I was going to be trapped at 30,000 feet with – another reminder of why spending time in Australia was going to be amazing.

The first leg of the journey was at night, which meant I spent most of the day of the flight second-guessing myself and wondering if I had everything packed. I like to be organised, which is why it took me so long to pack in the first place, but with the suitcase shut and the safety belt fastened around it (to stop the overloaded suitcase exploding and my underwear being scattered all across Sydney airport), I couldn't help doubting my packing skills. I had to resist the urge to unlock it and repack the whole thing, several times. Not that Buzz would've let me do so anyway. He was keeping me very busy that day, deciding to get up onto his feet, grab hold of his walker and storm across the room while giggling at his achievement. What a fantastic day to pick up a new skill and get moving more than ever – just before getting on a long-haul flight. He was going to love being contained for twenty-four hours. Not!

In the hope of keeping things as routine as possible, I fed and bathed Buzz at home at his normal times, before popping him in his PJs and into his car seat ready for the airport. In an ideal world he'd fall asleep in the taxi and remain that way until we were in the airport lounge and he could have a little play. Nope. Buzz did not like being in the strange car at night-time when he should be in bed, and wanted us all to know it by getting grizzly. But fear not, I was on it. I whipped out a packet of baby corn puffs and let him munch away on those, trying to stop my mind from frantically going through the list of the food for him I'd put in my hand luggage and working out whether it was going to be enough. It was. I had enough to feed every person on the flight, plus the ground crew at either end.

Not only was my suitcase meticulously packed, so was my hand luggage – which was arguably the most important of the two, as that was going to help me through whatever would be thrown at me over the next day. Thankfully I was allowed to take a couple of pieces of hand luggage onto the flight with us. So in one bag I had an endless supply of nappies, wipes and spare clothes (mostly for Buzz, but one top for me too as it was highly likely I was going to be getting all of Buzz's food down me), along with our passports and tickets, and in the other bag I had everything I could think of to entertain a baby. It was my bag of tricks – food, toys (some old, tried-and-tested reliable ones, the others new and interesting-looking), an iPad loaded with his favourite film *The Muppets* and loads of fun animal apps I'd found for babies (educational, don't you know), his headphones, and some books. I was as prepared as I was ever going to be for this flight. The rest was up to the gods . . . or Buzz.

Unsurprisingly our luggage was overweight when we got to the check-in desk . . . It was over 40 kilos! What on earth had I packed? Oh yes, all of Buzz's possessions. Thankfully Georgia and Izzy were both under, as it meant I could unload some of my baby crap onto them. It was a bit of a commotion (my underwear ended up being on show in Heathrow rather than Sydney), but before long we were making our way through security.

I had hoped that Buzz would sleep a little before we got onto the flight as it was past his bedtime, but he really fought hard and stayed awake – the intrigue of the airport keeping him alert and curious. This resulted in a few whiny moments here and there thanks to him being overtired, but before long we were in our seats and I gave him a little comfort feed to settle him down. Just like when we went to Italy, he was asleep before take-off. I took a deep breath and steeled myself for what was to come, yet I was thankful that we'd made it to our seat and that he was asleep – that bought everyone a little peace.

We were flying with Qantas, and on this particular aircraft, babies were given a little cot bed to sleep in; Buzz's was directly in front of my seat. I'd checked the measurements time and time again on the website, worried I'd be told he couldn't go in there because of his size and wondering what I'd do for such a long time if that were the case. It was a snug fit, and I was concerned he was too big for it, but when the flight attendant came over with sheets for me, she shrugged and said she'd seen bigger babies than Buzz in there. Fair enough. I was sold.

I popped my sleeping boy into the little cot with a sense of relief, feeling like I'd won the first battle.

The amazing thing about these travel cots was the woven seatbelts that clipped over the top to keep the baby secure, meaning you know there's absolutely no chance of them falling out – apparently it's even safe for them to stay in there during turbulence. It was very clever.

I should've made the most of having a sleeping baby and slept myself, but instead I made the most of having my own little TV screen and allowed myself to unwind a bit. I found myself watching *The Real Desperate Housewives of Melbourne.*

I get hooked on these sorts of reality shows as they always seem so over the top and wild, and as we'd be heading there, this felt like research. I watched one episode and then realised I was shattered, so reclined my chair and went to sleep.

Even though we were on a plane and there was nowhere he could go, I did have a moment of paranoia before closing my eyes. I've since wondered if every parent has this when flying – do we all sleep with one eye open or a hand placed across our child's body as protection against anything that might harm them?

As Buzz was at my feet I didn't have the reassurance of that physical connection, but my ears were still fine tuned to his cry, as I found out half an hour later, when he woke up in a complete panic. To be fair to him I'd have been the same if I'd gone to sleep in my loving mother's arms and woken up in some weird cage-like contraption somewhere I didn't know and was unable to move.

He calmed down quickly, but wanted to stay with me, his body bucking if I moved him so much as an inch from my body.

More episodes of *The Real Desperate Housewives of Melbourne* were watched while we snuggled and he slept on my lap – not the most comfortable thing, but he was happy and I was busy watching my guilty pleasure.

He slept for the majority of the first leg of the journey. When we landed in Dubai I was happy that he'd had a solid chunk of sleep, meaning he wouldn't be ridiculously tired when we continued with the longer half of the flight. We got off the plane, stretched our legs for a couple of hours, had some breakfast and went back to our seats.

The plane felt different this time. The lights were on for a start. It didn't feel all dark and cosy, it felt lively and busy. Buzz sat playing at my feet before take-off and charmed all the other passengers with his cheeky smile, something I was grateful for. At least that way they were aware he was adorable, cute and completely forgivable if he had a meltdown.

Now, I love a good routine, but I hadn't really thought about what to do with my sleep/feed schedules when flying across time zones. This was clearly an oversight, but it seemed to make sense to keep the first nap to two hours after him waking up.

It took me half an hour to rock him to sleep, yet he woke up as soon as I put him into the cot and had a huge meltdown. I scooped him up quickly and removed him from the seating area, taking him to a really quiet communal area I'd found which was empty and deciding to settle him once more there. This was purely because I didn't want the other passengers to be disgusted at me for making them put up with my screaming child when they'd paid a hefty fare for their plane ticket. I felt scrutinised, watched and judged and so scurried off as quick as I could, trying to solve the issue away from their eyes and ears.

It took me a further twenty minutes to calm Buzz down and get him back to sleep. But again, when I gently lowered him into his cot he woke up with a scream, clinging on to me in a total panic, as though I was about to abandon him.

That's when I cried in Georgia's arms while Izzy took Buzz for a tour of the aircraft, the exhaustion of the previous sleepless flight catching up with me, along with the feeling that I was letting everyone on the plane down. I know that sounds ridiculous, but that's how I felt as I buried my head in my hands and let the big fat tears fall.

That's when I had a little word with myself.

We were at 30,000 feet.

There were no rules.

Buzz didn't need to sleep in the bloody cot if he didn't want to. If all he wanted was to remain in my arms while in these strange, new surroundings then he wasn't asking for very much at all.

I took a deep breath, collected my child and then lovingly held him as he slept, managing to find a position in which we were both comfortable and could nap together.

That started a little loop of activity. We'd wake, have a little milk, then go back to the quiet communal area from earlier where I could put out his toys and he could crawl around; then we'd have some food, and then we'd nap again. The whole cycle took about two hours and would restart every time he woke up. At one point Izzy took him for a while, the two of them enjoying a cuddle while watching *The Muppets*. It was very cute to see.

It was while he was with her that I popped to the loo.

The woman who was seated behind me stopped and congratulated me, telling me I was doing a wonderful job. Not only that, but other passengers seemed more encouraging than they had previously. Once again (when will I learn?) I thought people were looking and thinking one thing, but they were actually thinking something else entirely. My presumptions about what they were thinking as they looked at me said more about me and my own paranoia and desire to get stuff right than it did about anyone else on that flight.

If I'd have realised that not everyone on that flight was against me, understood that some of them had travelled with kids before and knew what I was going through – that some of them would have been sympathetic – then I wouldn't have got myself into such a frenzy in the first place.

I always feel that there's no louder child than your own, but I don't think either of my boys actually had a monstrously loud cry, it just seems a thousand times more deafening when belted directly at your eardrum.

I was extremely thankful to the lady for her kindness and I now try to be just as warm and encouraging to other parents when getting on flights or even when I'm out in the supermarket and spot a tantrumming toddler. Moments like that can feel so isolating, especially when you're out of the house and feel like a fish in its tank being watched by a hovering hawk (I love a ridiculous metaphor). A little smile of acknowledgment or encouragement can work wonders to dissolve whatever is being felt. I like to think of it being my way of 'paying forward' the woman's kindness with some of my own.

We got to Sydney relatively unscathed in the end. I'd even go as far as to say I managed to enjoy our time in the sky. Nonetheless, I still couldn't wait to hand Buzz over to Tom and get some much-needed sleep when we got to the hotel!

20

EXPLORING WITH BUZZ

EXPLORING WITH BUZZ

lthough Tom and the McBusted boys were over in
Australia to perform and work, Buzz and I were there
to have an adventure. And that is what we did – sometimes with Tom (those were the best times), and sometimes
without. The nice thing was that Buzz and I could just get
on with our days and explore the wonderful cities we visited
without the need for a plan or schedule – especially on the
days we were in Sydney on our own while everyone else had
flown to Brisbane or Perth. This helped everything feel relaxed
and like a much-needed holiday. We had nothing to rush
around for – no classes, appointments or places to get to at
specific times. We could just *be*.

The day would always start the same, with breakfast down
in the hotel restaurant. We were invariably the first ones seated
thanks to Buzz being an early riser (with or without jet lag).
Occasionally we'd see the other guys and girls, but they usually
did what we would've done pre-Buzz and had room service

while lounging around in bed – or even having a lie-in and skipping breakfast altogether.

Scandalous.

For us, though, it was nice to get out of the room and see somewhere beyond those four walls. Plus the buffet cart of fruit, pastries, bread and cereals cut out having to wait for food to arrive, which stopped Buzz getting grouchy with hunger. No one wants a baby meltdown before they've had their first cup of coffee in the morning.

Our chosen routine was a lovely way of starting the day all together. While Tom was with us (and not in Brisbane or Perth) it was something we always did thanks to it happening so early in the day – sometimes we'd even get a little walk in too before Tom needed to go to work. That was always nice.

We walked a lot. I would pop Buzz into his Mountain Nano (a flipping amazing lightweight, compact buggy to use when travelling), velcro a little caddy organiser onto the back containing everything I might need so it was retrievable within seconds (high-factor suntan lotion, glasses, snacks, hat, money, camera, phone, a Lamaze toy to dangle off his straps) and we'd be off to find some fun. Some days we'd head out to the shops, or to the park for a picnic, or we'd get on a ferry to the zoo or Manly – anywhere the wind blew us.

I loved going out for lunch with Buzz. There was a gorgeous little restaurant called Metro St James on the edge of Hyde Park that served delicious stone-baked pizzas. I'd get us a margherita to share and we'd sit there munching away while watching people coming and going. I was always amazed at how calm it felt sitting doing something rather grown up with a baby – but that's Buzz for you. He absolutely loves his food so he's in his element when there's a plate of food in front of him. One day we even went for a picnic in the Royal Botanic Gardens, finding a scenic spot in the shade with the most amazing view of the Sydney Opera House. We sat there, had some lunch and soaked up the beautiful view before us. It was nice to have those moments of calmness with Buzz when I was used to always being run ragged and having a million things on. Obviously he still ran me ragged, but I found myself enjoying his company so much more during the trip. I'm not saying I didn't usually enjoy it (although some of the testier moments I could have done without), but just that things were completely different over there when my main focus was simply being his mum.

Buzz's favourite place to go was the Sea Life aquarium, which was only a ten-minute walk from where we were staying in Darling Harbour. I think we went there three or four times.

He just loved the tunnels down the bottom where the big rays and sharks would swim over us. I found it slightly petrifying, if I'm honest, but he loved it and would remain captivated for ages, his curious eyes full of wonder as they followed the creatures gliding around the tank. I'd point things out to him as they swam over us, but really I loved just looking at him and the endless expressions twitching across his pretty face.

That's something I've found myself doing a lot since becoming a mum – whenever we're somewhere new or they're experiencing something for the first time (or second, third, fourth, or fifth . . .), I turn to the boys to see their reactions. I love it. It's like looking at the world with a fresh set of eyes; all that innocence and intrigue as they soak up the sights in front of them is so beautiful. It makes me see how wonderful the world outside can be if we're open to seeing it without judgment or prejudice.

I could clearly see Buzz loved the aquarium and therefore loved going back time and time again, even if it was just for an hour at a time. It made sense to me to do things that Buzz enjoyed doing. After all, it was his holiday as well as mine and I had no real big desire to go anywhere in particular.

Although we were somewhere new and exciting, sometimes it was also nice to just chill out at the hotel with the bag of toys I'd taken over there for him so that he could have a proper crawl around rather than being restricted by his buggy or baby carrier, where he was forced to sit still while I took him from place to place.

That was the only downside to him not being able to walk yet.

I just made sure I balanced our days, with a trip out in the morning then a nap in his cot at the hotel (or on the move if I had a big trip planned), before spending the afternoon at the hotel either playing in the room, corridors or lobby, or heading out for a swim – an activity he loved.

Being outside did freak me out thanks to my concerns about the weather. Pre-Buzz I'd have been praying for blazing hot days where I could recline on a sunlounger and soak up the rays to ensure I went home fifty shades darker than I was when I left, but I've found it completely different with a baby in tow.

Even now, whenever the sun decides to pop out with his hat on and declare he's ready to play, I experience a mild panic, shielding the boys from the harmful rays glaring down on us while running a mental check of everything I might need to do to ensure they don't get heat stroke or burnt. I then spend the whole day giving them copious amounts of water so that they don't dehydrate and staring at their skin to see if the lotion I've smothered them in is doing its job properly. My beady eyes searching for the dreaded patch of red . . . I'm sure I'm not the only mum to be like this when it comes to these matters, although I will accept that I am probably overly paranoid about it.

I can remember going on holiday to Tenerife as a kid and having so much fun in the pool that I completely burned my shoulders and the backs of my knees. I stayed in the hotel room the following day with ice-packs laid out on top of me. The day after that I had to go out wearing 'the T-shirt of shame', letting all the other holidaymakers know I'd been a fool. And that's me, who has quite olive skin. I've had other tanning disasters too where I've missed patches (like a thin line down my nose, a patch on my leg, my entire chest), so I know I can be a bit slapdash when it comes to sunscreen. That was something I definitely didn't want happening in Australia to Buzz. I would've been mortified.

Thankfully I was mostly in luck while we were over there, as it didn't get as hot as I know it can. There were hotter days, of course, but on the whole it was quite cloudy. Don't worry, I still made sure I applied the sunscreen. I know those pesky rays like to frazzle the unprepared on an overcast day – I learned that lesson on a trip to Lanzarote where the wind blew up a right mare. I told you I was terrible . . .

· · · · ·

While we didn't go along to every show the boys played, we did go along to some. As they were playing in stadiums they were always brilliant to see, despite backstage never being as fun as what people might imagine – something that was even truer on this trip thanks to a baby and a breastfeeding mum being present. Saying that, having boobs swinging free in a dressing room is quite rock and roll, so maybe I should retract that comment.

The nice thing about going along on tour was that the boys and girls got to see Buzz, and Buzz them. We used to see each other all the time years ago thanks to us being neighbours, but life moved on and people moved away, leaving Tom and I to be the only ones remaining in the 'McFly Village'. Because of that no one had really spent that much time with Buzz, so it was heartwarming to see him with some of our best friends and for them to be enjoying his company.

There's a real pride that comes with the knowledge that your friends think your child is cool and funny, a feeling I hadn't realised even existed. Buzz was brilliant for the entire trip (thanks to us always having water and snacks on hand). I'd even go as far as to say he made touring with a baby look easy.

I think Harry said at one point that he'd never seen Buzz cry.

This made me laugh a lot. Probably more than I should have. I didn't bother correcting him and just took the compliment.

I'm not entirely sure what Buzz made of the shows while he sat and watched with his big ear defenders on. It wasn't the first time he'd seen Tom onstage – I'd actually had him with me when the boys headlined at Hyde Park, too – but he'd only been four months then and paid more attention to my best friend Katy who was dancing for him during the whole show, much to his delight.

He was more aware by eleven months, so I was looking forward to seeing his reaction. I always popped him in the baby carrier so that he was fastened to me and in no risk of going anywhere, then I'd bounce around to the music and swing his arms in the air as he laughed along. The other girls loved making a fuss of him too, pointing out where Tom was to see if he understood. He'd just frown back while taking it all in – not confirming or denying that he knew it was his dada up onstage. There were also times he'd just conk out during a set.

With so much going on it was hardly surprising he got tired!

21
BEING A MUM CAN GIVE YOU FOMO

BEING A MUM CAN GIVE YOU FOMO

It was a very odd feeling when Tom and the rest of the group left me and Buzz in Sydney. The city suddenly felt bigger, emptier and quieter because I'd lost all my friends and the crew who'd come along. It went from being a group excursion to a trip for two – and even though it had been mainly us two for a large part of it anyway, with everyone gone, it made it feel even more like we were alone. We'd walk down for breakfast knowing there was absolutely no chance of bumping into anyone we knew, and the same was true of the pool and the lift lobby (always a good place for people to congregate).

It was just us.

That's not to say I felt distressed at the thought of being miles away from home in a foreign country on my own with Buzz. Clearly the fact everyone spoke English was a huge help. I imagine I'd have felt completely different if I had been left in a non-English-speaking country and unable to communicate with anyone.

Every single person I met, from the hotel staff to people on the street, was so warm, friendly and welcoming, and it was being in that company in those gorgeous surroundings that had me feeling light and giddy about the adventure I was having with my son.

But it took some mental adjustment when the others left, that's all – although it did mean I could get some good sleep in by going to bed when Buzz did, and actually doing a little work when Buzz had his naps.

On that note, I don't think I did any actual writing while I was away, and I was meant to be working on my third novel, *Dream a Little Dream*. It's something my editor was well aware of and totally fine about, so I don't mind sharing that with you. I had the best of intentions and had a great plan in my head, but when I was over there that plan dissipated.

It's not every day you find yourself in Australia, so the notion of word counts and handover dates absconded from my brain. I also think that on a trip like the one I was on you should be free to explore and just be, without being bogged down by normal life. Obviously this is easier said than done when you're months away from a deadline, but writing is really the coming together of observations, of bringing to life different parts of your imagination and creativity. Being somewhere new and meeting people from other walks of life is important . . . well, that's my excuse, anyway, and I'm sticking to it. I got the work done in the end (and I was very pleased with the book I produced) while managing to have a great trip away with my family too. I'd say it was a win-win situation.

With the group gone I did occasionally find myself thinking

about what they were all up to. I got that feeling we've all experienced when taking a sick day from school – you feel great at first as you snuggle under your duvet and enjoy the extra bit of sleep, followed by some *Jeremy Kyle* in the background while you munch on toast. But by first break you find yourself wondering what you're missing out on and are eager to be back in class – a classic example of FOMO (fear of missing out).

Obviously Tom was constantly in touch with us and making sure we were fine, but there were moments when I felt a little out of the loop with the rest of group.

Izzy, Georgia and Ellie were great at pre-empting this and made a real effort to keep me involved by messaging me every day and seeing what we were up to – as though we were missed. It probably sounds a silly thing to be thankful for, but a year earlier and I'd have been with them all, going for casual shopping trips, heading to the beach or lounging by the pool. My trip over there was vastly different because I'd become a mum and had a new set of responsibilities and a baby who needed to stick to some sort of a routine, and had to have his own needs met before I could fulfill my own.

In hindsight it could've been quite isolating, but I found myself getting lost in the wonderful city. Besides, I was far from alone – I had the best company ever.

. . . . .

After a few days alone in Sydney it was time for me to do my first ever solo flight with Buzz and fly to Melbourne. It was all running smoothly because I was super organised, but there were a few moments when I realised having two sets of hands is most definitely better than one – the first being when I had to go through security and the officers wanted me to collapse the buggy and put it through the scanners. That was a two-handed job and I had Buzz on my hip. I ended up handing him over to a flight attendant while I quickly pressed a few buttons and folded the pram down. She looked trustworthy and we were surrounded by security, so I felt safe about doing it.

The next time I needed help was disembarking at Melbourne, when I needed to get the pram and my rucksack down from the overhead compartment. The lovely chap next to me took Buzz while I grabbed it all.

Actually, the guy I ended up sitting next to on that flight was lovely. Even though the more I flew with Buzz the less afraid of it I was, I was still worried about upsetting other passengers (old habits). So I decided to follow my mantra 'kill it with kindness'. It works in every aspect of life . . . usually. Anyway, I walked onto the plane and found we were seated next to a man in his thirties, so I turned to him and said, 'Oh no, you've pulled the short straw, I'm afraid – you're sat with me and a baby.' He laughed and thankfully this broke the ice. It turned out that he also had a little boy around Buzz's age and wasn't fazed in the slightest. I was so relieved. Especially as Buzz wouldn't stop tapping him and playing with his watch.

Buzz was really well behaved on this flight. It was his naptime a little while after we got on, so once we'd taken off I carried him to the back of the plane and rocked him to sleep. He then slept on me for a good hour or so, and spent another hour eating. It really was getting easier the more I flew with him – although I made a mental note to wear my carrier for the next solo flight with him a few days later.

I've yet to do a flight with both boys on my own. I doubt I will while they're still so young (I mean, is it possible to get one adult and two children into a plane loo if one of you needs to go?), but I have found that organisation when travelling anywhere is key, even on a simple trip to the shops.

· · ● · ·

It was lovely being reunited with the gang in Melbourne. The guys and gals were all waiting for us when we arrived. Actually, they were standing in a queue to buy juices, but it was still nice to see them all and to know they felt the same in return. My FOMO was unnecessary. Nothing particularly out of the ordinary had happened.

Lesson learned.

Our time in Australia was disjointed, with us going from Sydney to Melbourne, then Adelaide, then Sydney again before heading back to Melbourne and flying home. Although I loved the comfort of getting to know one hotel and one city, it was brilliant to be able to see more than one place and get around Australia a bit.

Adelaide was the biggest surprise for me as I hadn't really known much about it. It's a lot less condensed than Sydney and Melbourne, with wide-open spaces and not much height to it in terms of skyscrapers (I don't remember there being any). It felt good to see nature again after being in the city centre of Melbourne for a few days.

I completely fell in love with our new surroundings and found it a shame we were only there for a couple of nights.

A new city brought with it a new hotel, and there was one thing I loved doing every time we entered our new room: a thorough risk assessment. With Buzz on the move it seemed he was on a mission to hunt out any danger. Plug sockets, cables, sharp corners – I had to make sure I found them all before he did. The hotels must've thought I was bonkers because I was constantly rearranging furniture to make it softer around the edges. I did make sure I put it back before I left, though – if I could remember where it all went!

Blooming baby brain.

· · · · ·

Talking of Buzz being on the move, one of the first things we did when we arrived in Sydney was travel to a department store and buy Buzz a new walker, seeing as we couldn't take our clunky wooden one over there with us. I was going to be staying in the one place for a good chunk of time, so I wanted Buzz to keep having fun with his walker now that he had discovered how to use it.

Not content with bashing his new Thomas the Tank Engine walker (it looked like a train but he could sit on it or walk behind it) into the walls of our room, Buzz used to venture out into the hallway between all of our rooms, which gave him the biggest runway to travel along ever. He had lots of fun tottering around and his confidence on his feet really grew. So much so that he took his first step in Melbourne, an hour before we were due to fly home.

Despite our fears, he didn't spend the whole flight running up and down the aisles annoying everyone else on board. He didn't increase the effort until a few weeks later – when we were in Newcastle on the McBusted tour. A group of us were backstage trying to encourage him with lots of whooping and cheering. He found it so funny. Enjoying the attention he was

One of Buddy's first smiles. I have a feeling he was meant to be sleeping.

Buddy, shot by Buzz. Candid photography at its best!

Each morning I used to grab Buzz's bag of toys and place each one around him in a circle, telling him what they were as I went. He was in the army crawl stage by this point, and just used to shuffle from one toy to the next.

Buzz dressed as Woody. Oh, the irony. I'm dressed as The Snowman, obviously. I was a couple of months pregnant here, thankfully my snowman costume disguised my bloated tummy.

When Buzz met Buzz.

Like father like son . . . Buzz has always been interested in music. He usually watches Tom in awe before having a bash himself.

Buzz on stage during sound check with his daddy and his mates. He cried so much when it was over, so we went back the following day. He talks about it all the time.

Buddy. Those lips, those cheeks, that face...

These two love rolling around together. I imagine it's going to
get a bit louder and more 'enthusiastic' as time goes on.

Hanging out in Adelaide with Buzz. As you can see, I made sure he was totally covered up!

Buzz rocking my sunnies far better than I do!

Buzz first thing in the morning. I'm thrilled to say he's a tidier eater these days.

Buzz stopping to smell the flowers. I love this picture – it gives me a little reminder to do the same every time I see it.

Trip to the theatre with Buzz to see Tom's *Dinosaur that Pooped* picture book series on stage. Buzz was blown away when he met Dino afterwards.

Little Miss Summer Rae, my niece. The love I feel
towards her is limitless, much like the love I have for my own children.
I can't wait to see them all playing together in a year or so.

Buzz grew two inches in two months
… I couldn't believe it. Although, Tom
also grew an inch, so maybe I'm not
very good at measuring. Ha!

Tom and Buzz sitting behind me and
chilling with a beverage while I'm
trying to get some work done.

My loves!

receiving, he just went for it – giving us a whole nine steps in one go. It was an emotional moment.

Milestones like that always arouse a mixture of emotions in me. Pride is obviously the first thing I feel, a sense of elation that the little human we're helping to grow has achieved something that will help him to thrive and develop further in life, but then there is an element of sadness, too; a hole forming in my heart at the fact that a change is occurring, reminding me that they won't just stay little and innocent forever. That eventually I'll stop being needed quite so much.

That's pretty heartbreaking.

A couple of days ago I watched Tom teach Buzz how to hold a pencil; he then helped him write out his name over some dot-to-dots I'd drawn. My little boy understood what he was doing. He was engaged and visibly wanting to learn. The sight totally choked me up, leaving me to fight back the tears that threatened to spill. It felt like such a poignant moment, perhaps because Tom and I both write for a living and this was the very start of developing those writing skills. Who knows. Emotions when you're a mum can be so topsy-turvy. I'm constantly surprised by a rush of emotion at the simplest of things – Buzz eating with a spoon, putting his own socks on, putting toys away, or pretending to express (I was slightly mortified here too but luckily nothing was attached to the pump).

At two years and eight months old, Buzz continues to blow me away with his knowledge, awareness and playful attitude towards life. What makes me most proud is seeing how much love he displays for his little brother. Watching him as he goes to Buddy and kisses his cheek for no other reason than that he wants to, is beyond moving.

Buddy absolutely adores his big brother back and watches his every move, as though he's soaking up the information for his own development. I'm pretty sure this is why he's desperate to walk already. Crawling just isn't cutting it for him so, at eight months, he's been up on his feet and attempting to use the walker. It's frightening how quickly Buddy seems to be progressing, but that's part of being a second child – he just wants to be doing everything Buzz is.

I'm sure they'll fight when they get older, all siblings do, but I hope they'll also have a bond that'll see them through anything life might throw at them – just like I do with Giorgie and Mario.

22
JET LAG IS A BITCH

JET LAG IS A BITCH

There's been something I've neglected to share during this whole Australia section and that is sleep, or the lack of it.

You might recall me saying that I rocked Buzz to sleep when we were on the plane from England to ensure he got his naps in and didn't get overtired. Well, I continued giving him a helping hand for the first few days so that he could work through his jet lag without too much of a struggle. It seemed the most sensible thing to do to help him get back into a routine.

Actually, giving him a helping hand became a bit of a necessity as we were all staying in the one hotel room, with his cot placed right next to our bed. Given the chance he would've happily just sat and watched Tom and me, even if we were just sitting at our laptops getting on with work. So we'd put Norah Jones on (I listened to 'Come Away With Me' every day when I was pregnant with him and it subsequently helped him drift off), give him a cuddle and gently rock him to sleep. We'd then whip out our headphone splitter and watch *Better Call Saul* or *Broadchurch* with a glass of wine in hand – possibly even a little dark chocolate if we were really treating ourselves.

It would've been great if Buzz had remained asleep until the following morning, but he rarely did while we were over there. I don't think he did at all, actually. He'd stay quiet until just after midnight, and then would be constantly up throughout the night.

He was teething around this time too, so that didn't help matters either.

Bloody teeth!

I did find some great biscuits while we were in Oz (the band's driver told me about them). They were called Rafferty's Garden Banana Milk Teething Rusks and were the hardest things ever. Seriously – I thought I'd have a nibble on one to see what they were like and nearly cracked a tooth. They clearly helped Buzz, though, as he loved munching on them. Sadly they don't sell them over here as I've been desperate to get some for Buddy and haven't found anything like them yet.

But back to sleep . . . I'm well aware that something you kiss goodbye to as soon as you become a parent is a good night's sleep, but somehow you get used to the disruptions and adapt. Bizarrely, you even feel fully functional when waking up in the mornings having had little to no sleep (something I'm really experiencing now with Buddy, who hasn't gone back to sleeping through the night after his four-month sleep regression – wah!). However, by that point in Oz Buzz had been sleeping through the night for months. He was a brilliant sleeper and able to self-settle too – meaning we used to give him a kiss and a cuddle, say goodnight and leave him to put himself to sleep. The jet lag and the fact we were somewhere new blew apart our well-established nightly routine, causing all our hard work to go to pot.

It's fair to say the return of the nightly chaos was a complete shock to our systems, and really wasn't helped by our own jet lag. Buzz would wake up highly distressed because he was so shattered. I'd feed him and try to put him back into his cot when he eventually fell back asleep, but it was just like it had been on the plane. He'd wake up as soon as his head touched the mattress, grabbing hold of me in a panic and giving me a look of disbelief, unable to fathom why I'd be so cruel as to put him down into the safety and comfort of a cot when he was loving being in my arms so much.

He'd cry a lot then, his emotions giving way to full-on meltdowns. It was horrible. He was so happy and fun the rest of the trip but with the darkness of the nights came a completely different child.

While alone with him in Sydney, it all got a little too much one night and I ended up having a mini-breakdown of my own. He was resisting sleep and angrily screaming in my face while he did so. It felt relentless. I was so frazzled as I stood there, bouncing on the spot, struggling to keep my eyes open while singing 'Life's a Happy Song' from *The Muppets* on repeat. My sleepy interpretation managed to lose anything that sounded like a melody – the words jumbled and wrong. No wonder Buzz kept crying; I sounded awful.

That pitiful version stuck around for the rest of the trip – with Tom stopping me one night and asking what on earth I was singing. The song we listened to at least a dozen times a day had become completely unrecognisable. That's what exhaustion had done to me.

After I found my own sobs blending in with Buzz's, I did

something we hadn't done before. I let him into my bed, because he was fine as long as he was in my arms but would panic and cry if I tried to put him elsewhere. My solution seemed to make perfect sense.

I never really co-slept when Buzz was a baby. The mesh side of his SnuzPod crib allowed me to stare at him all I wanted, but also gave me the security of knowing I wasn't about to roll onto him in my sleep or suffocate him with my duvet or pillows. It felt safer for me. I'm not against co-sleeping, I think it's a lovely thing for families to do, but I was simply too paranoid to do it with a newborn. By eleven months old, though, Buzz was sturdier. I felt it would be pretty difficult to miss his solid frame in the bed, so it quickly became an extremely tempting option when I could no longer keep my eyes open and was struggling to stay upright. It was something I struggled over, but given the circumstances, I reasoned with myself that sleep of any kind was better than no sleep. FOR BOTH OF US! And if all Buzz wanted was a little cuddle from me to know I was there, then I was more than happy to comply with that demand. I'm his mummy, after all. It's my role to be that beacon of comfort. In all honesty, it was actually really lovely to feel his hand holding onto my arm, or the weight of his sleeping body against mine. It felt naughty because it wasn't something we'd done before, but I instantly saw the appeal. It was lovely being that close.

I was worried that he'd fall out of bed, so I put him in the middle, moved myself closer to the edge and then placed pillows on what would've been Tom's side as well as on the floor. I also decreased my own pillow usage from two to one so that there wasn't anything too bulky around – I'd completed a quick midnight risk assessment. Funnily enough, neither of us moved much during the night anyway, and if we did I was extremely aware of it.

The happy look on Buzz's face when he woke up in the morning and realised he was with me was magical. What a perfect few hours of snuggling we had. There was no denying the fact he'd slept for longer than normal because he'd been in with me.

From then on each night, whether Tom was with us or not, we'd settle Buzz into his cot at the start of his bedtime knowing that a few hours later we'd eventually find him in with us. We were away from home and only metres away from him in bed. I didn't see a problem with it. It would've felt bizarre, cruel and pointless to do anything else, when putting him in with us kept everything nice and calm.

How were we to know the impact that decision was to have on our lives. How naïve we were. How innocent and foolish . . .

23

MAKING A BIG FLIPPING ROD

MAKING A BIG FLIPPING ROD

continually hear the term 'making a rod for your own back' in discussions about motherhood, with people warning others not to do certain things with their child because it'll almost definitely cause difficulties somewhere down the line. Picking up your baby when they cry, allowing your baby to sleep on you or giving them a dummy are just a few examples of the things people with more experience (or bigger and more vocal gobs) than you like to advise you about.

One of the circumstances in which I heard that saying used was when children's sleeping habits – and more specifically, allowing your child to sleep in your bed – were discussed on *Loose Women* (I watched far too much daytime TV while on maternity leave with Buzz), with all the ladies on the panel presenting their own, very different, stances on the matter. At that point we were lucky to have a child who slept in his own bed, but that didn't mean I felt he'd be banned from our bedroom forever more. I loved the thought of us all snuggled under the duvet on a cold, wintry Sunday morning – perhaps munching on a communal breakfast in bed.

I was surprised to find there was such an aversion to it, but as always, I try not to judge others for their opinions and I'm sure they were just doing what worked for them and their family. It was none of my business, but interesting to hear different viewpoints being shared nonetheless.

The jet lag when we got home was terrible, but we were faced with a far bigger problem – getting Buzz to sleep in his cot, or even to self-settle. If I put him down in his bed and left the room, as we had been doing for months and months before heading to Australia, he would go crazy.

Like batshit crazy, crazy.

He would scream and cry until he was blue in the face, desperate for me to be back in there with him. As though the idea of being alone in there was awful.

It was horrific.

A couple of times I tried standing outside his room and giving him a few minutes to calm down, in the hope that he'd realise he was fine and remember that he was in a room that he'd previously loved. It just didn't work. I'd watch him on the video monitor while fighting back the tears myself, hating the fact he was so distressed. I'd walk back in to find him soaked with sweat, his body shaking as though he'd just suffered a great ordeal.

In his world, and in his innocent little mind, he had.

In those moments, when he wrapped his arms around my neck and held on tightly – fearful that I might leave him again – I didn't care what any book or sleep expert had to say on the matter. I was happy to hug him to sleep. To calm him down and let him know he was safe, and that there was nothing to worry about. I'd shush in his ear before whispering words of love, promising I'd never let him cry like that again. Hating the fact that I had.

Let's remember he'd just spent a solid three weeks by my side. We had been inseparable, with us literally in the same breathing space for the entire trip to Oz. It's not surprising he wasn't up for the idea of suddenly being away from me and left on his own. Three weeks might not seem like a huge amount of time for an adult, but it must feel like a lifetime for one so young.

I'm sure some experts out there would claim I'd been played and had been manipulated into caving in to the demands of my baby when I should've been firmer. Well screw that. I was more than happy to let him win that battle and get what he wanted. Winning myself would've majorly sucked balls.

Big ones.

Sadly, rocking Buzz to sleep had become a bit more of a workout thanks to him getting bigger, therefore it got pretty knackering when he fought it or would wake up as soon as I lowered him into bed.

I have clear memories of trying to lower him down as though he was a feather, gently floating him from side to side in the imaginary breeze before softly landing on his mattress. Sometimes that would work; other times his eyes would ping open as soon as he felt my hand pull away from beneath him. Or my ankle or knee would make a snapping sound as I tried to leave the room.

I'd suck in my breath, as suspense filled the room. Willing Buzz to stay asleep and remain oblivious to the creaking my body had made. More often than not he'd wake up, rolling over to find me and investigate what I was up to before giving a whimper, the process starting once again.

I used to count a lot in those moments. I'd tell myself to bounce with him for sixty seconds with my eyes shut, sure that he'd be asleep when I next opened my eyes. When I could feel he was still resisting I'd increase the target to one hundred or start all over again, the repetitive beat in my head getting me through, making me feel like I was coming closer to having a successfully sleeping child.

I probably should've used the time wisely and spent it thinking through projects I was working on or planning dinner; anything would've been more productive than the numbers building in my brain.

It was a lot like counting to ten to relax, just a much longer version of it.

· · ▪ · ·

That was just getting him to bed. The next dilemma was keeping him there during the night.

Buzz had now experienced life in bed with his mummy and daddy, so he knew exactly what he was missing. When he woke in the night he kept on crying, his body leaning over towards his bedroom door, letting me know exactly what he wanted.

Our bed.

So in he came, ready to completely take over my side.

It's a wonder I've never rolled out, seeing as I'm only ever left with six inches of mattress to lie on.

During those snuggles Buzz made his status as a mummy's boy very clear. It was me he wanted. If Tom tried to cuddle him or give him a kiss he'd wriggle away with a moan, nuzzling closer into me. Having experienced it the other way round I know how heartbreaking it must've been for Tom. But I was always envious as I lay there, looking at Tom sleeping soundly while Buzz continually pinched me in his sleep.

Argh, his pinching was the most irritating thing ever. It blooming hurt.

He'd get into the creases of my elbows, the back of my arms or the thinner skin around my neck. He used to do it when he was really little, but it became a more definite source of comfort the older he became. It was like torture.

Most of the time I'd gently brush his hands away to try and get him to stop.

It didn't always work.

Occasionally I'd try and hide any piece of upper-body flesh by wearing a long-sleeved roll neck to bed.

It didn't always work.

Other times I'd just let him pinch me even though it made me cry, because I could see it was helping him sleep. And that meant we got to too.

We knew we had to do something to get him out of this phase of getting into our bed, but when we got back from our travels we only had a week or so at home before the UK leg of the McBusted tour started. We were going to be back in hotel rooms, so figured there wasn't much point trying to break the bonkers routine we'd got ourselves into. We felt it was worth just sticking to what got us all some sleep until we knew we were going to be back at home and things would be returning to normal. We just rolled with it, because there really didn't seem to be much point in doing anything else when it was going to cause so many unnecessary tears. Not when I had a book to write and Tom had rehearsals to go to – we needed sleep so that we could function properly and do our jobs.

24
MOTHER TO A ONE-YEAR-OLD

MOTHER TO A ONE-YEAR-OLD

Seeing as Buzz was turning one while Tom was on tour in Scotland, we decided to go along for the first leg of it and visit Glasgow, Newcastle and Leeds, so that Buzz would be with his daddy on the special day. That being said, we figured a birthday party wasn't a birthday party without also seeing our family, so he actually had a little get-together at home before we left, too. We invited both our immediate families and Tom's grandparents, Joan and Ken. That's it.

We'd just got back from Australia and were in chaos before the start of the tour (unsurprisingly we had a backlog of chores to get on with after three weeks away), so we decided not to have a big children's party and keep it calm and intimate instead. I felt guilty for not throwing Buzz the biggest ever party and going mad with decorations, children's entertainers and lots of craziness, but to be honest he didn't really have many friends his age and I reasoned that he was only one and wouldn't even remember it. The people he saw all the time were our families, so having them over causing a fuss would be enough of an occasion for him.

The night before his birthday party at home we blew up lots of balloons, hung up 'Happy Birthday' banners and rearranged all the frames on our picture wall in the lounge to contain pictures of his favourite characters from *The Muppets*, *Peppa Pig* and *Mickey Mouse Clubhouse* (these pictures actually stayed up there for months and months afterwards because we kept forgetting to take them down). Tom's Uncle Arthur's sister-in-law Edith, who we've never actually met, kindly offered to make him a special *Toy Story* cake for the occasion, which was very sweet and thoughtful of her (I can confirm that it tasted delicious).

It was a lovely chilled-out day, and although it will slip from his memory, I can tell you that Buzz spent the entire time laughing a lot while enjoying his first ever bit of cake (thanks Edith!).

Even though we'd had that celebration at home I knew I wanted to do something for him on his actual birthday. First things first I went on Google and looked for a good cake company up in Glasgow. Buzz had to have a cake on his birthday. Plus, I knew exactly what I wanted him to have – the same Kermit cake Walter has in the opening sequence of *The Muppets*. I stumbled across a bakery called The Little Cake Parlour. The website looked as fab as their cakes, so I got in touch with them to see if they could help.

I knew nothing about the company, and hadn't gone to them off the back of a recommendation, only from their beautiful website, so it was a risky move to take. I was a bit apprehensive about what was going to turn up to be honest, but the cake waiting for us when we arrived at the hotel was wonderful, as were the little cupcakes of other *Muppet* characters they'd made. I literally couldn't have been more impressed.

We were staying not far from Glasgow in Mar Hall, an Edwardian hotel in a beautiful countryside setting, a scenic spot for a very special day.

The morning of his birthday we woke up and presented Buzz with his mini-pile of presents. We hadn't gone mad buying a ridiculous amount of stuff for the sake of it. Instead we bought him a few items we knew he'd enjoy, like a little animal puzzle, a hammer and peg wooden toy, a packet of Mega Bloks and a boat for the bath (he still absolutely loves spending time in there).

It was a chilled-out morning with us heading for breakfast and going out for a walk. Then in the afternoon, after his nap, we arranged for an afternoon tea celebration with the rest of the group.

I've got the cutest picture of Buzz in a party hat, looking extremely happy as he chomped on some food. But the celebrations didn't stop there. That night I decided to take him along to a McBusted concert. The shows in Australia had been outdoor ones, so I knew this one at the Hydro Arena was going to feel completely different for him. It would be louder for a start, which wasn't a problem as he had his ear defenders on, but the sound waves almost hit you in that environment, making it a little more intense. Still, I knew he'd be fine watching, as he'd be in his carrier with me and away from the crowds, therefore he wouldn't feel too overwhelmed. In fact, I thought he'd fall asleep after the first few songs, but he didn't. He stayed awake for the whole thing, mesmerised by what was happening onstage and the audience's reaction to it – all the while desperately waving at his daddy. He loved it.

Whenever Tom is onstage and spots me in the crowd, I always feel a little spark of magic, which I know is silly because he's my husband and it makes me feel a bit more like a fan (when I was fifteen I went to see *Boogie Nights* and I swear my heart stopped when Will Mellor looked at me) – but there's something special about there being thousands of people in the room and his eyes landing on mine. Tom used to seek me out during 'All About You' (a song he wrote for me as a Valentine's gift, which then went on to make millions of pounds for Comic Relief back in 2005) and sing it to me. It was pretty romantic. However, having Tom spot Buzz waving at him and seeing him wave back completely topped it. Time almost slows down in moments like that. It was epic, and I even shed a little tear.

Talking of me and my emotions . . . I found having my baby turn one created a swell of feelings, forcing me to reflect on how far I'd come since cack-handedly trying to feed him in the hospital and then us nervously taking him home.

Huge changes had occurred since he found himself 'on the outside', and I seriously didn't feel like the same person I'd been before he arrived. Perhaps it was only due to the lack of sleep, or the fact I no longer showered or pooped alone, but there was no denying that life had altered. Things that had seemed to worry or stress me out before no longer did; I was too busy fretting over the colour and texture of baby poop (seriously fascinating stuff). Or wondering when would be a good time to cut out the 5 p.m. nap, introduce real food, or go up a size in baby clothes. All of which demanded my attention – something my pre-baby self would've found hilarious.

My perception of what's important has shifted dramatically – even more so as I get older and as I move further along in this journey of motherhood.

Since I was five months pregnant with Buzz, I've written weekly blogs for *Hello!* online. I love having these posts to look back on, which is something I do from time to time, simply because I can't believe time is slipping away so quickly and I like remembering how I felt in certain moments. Blogging has been wonderful for me. It's been lovely to sit down with my thoughts each week and just share how I'm feeling. Sometimes they're more like diaries, in the sense of me detailing what I was up to that week, but other times they're more personal, with me opening up about what's affecting my heart in that particular moment. I wrote a blog on reaching the big milestone of Buzz's first birthday. I love reading it, so I'm going to share it with you:

Buzz is now a one-year-old . . . it feels so odd typing that. It's been an extremely emotional week for me as I've found myself reminiscing about this time last year, when he first entered our lives.

The last year has been filled with so many different emotions. I think I've laughed, cried and loved more than I have in my entire lifetime. Being a mum is hard work – I can't remember the last time I had a lie-in or showered without feeling like I had to rush in case Buzz woke up or, if showering before Tom goes to work, didn't hurry so that we both had time to get ready before he left. Holding conversations and dining out with friends has become a multi-tasking mission that's exhausting as you listen and nod eagerly (loving the adult interaction) while simultaneously jumping at your child's every move and dragging them away from plug sockets and sharp edges on tables, and removing from their mouths whatever it is they found and started chewing on while you picked up your coffee cup for a quick swig of its lukewarm contents. And then there's my appearance. I permanently look as though I've just got out of bed in my frumpy, bedraggled state – yet if only that were the case, since as I stated above, I haven't slept in for a whole year now . . . In fact, I can't even remember the last time I slept the whole way through the night – because, even if Buzz does, I can't help but go in and check up on him.

Gone are the days when I could spend hours getting ready; gone are the hot drinks and the hours of sleep. Gone are the endless episodes of trashy TV (they've been replaced with The Muppets *on repeat). Gone is my size ten figure (for now).*

Yet . . . I don't care.

I'm perfectly happy with this new way of living – especially when Buzz cracks a smile in my direction, laughs at something stupid I'm doing for his amusement, sings along to whatever I'm squawking to or gives me a kiss I've not had to ask for. Those are the magical moments that make everything worthwhile and remind me how beautiful my life has become.

'We made him.'

Those are the words that we've said dozens of times over the last year as we've watched in amazement as he's tackled the world around him. In many ways it feels as though it was only yesterday that we welcomed him into our lives, but in others it feels as though he's always been here with us.

I feel immensely proud to have such a gorgeous little boy to call my son.

It makes me want to weep reading that, partly because I can remember all those feelings swirling around me when I wrote it, but also because we've come even further since then with the arrival of our Buddy – who will have celebrated his own first birthday by the time this is published.

OK, those tears that were threatening to spill have now escaped, because that really is quite something.

25

I WILL RECLAIM MY SLEEPING HOURS

(OR, I'LL NEVER SLEEP AGAIN)

I WILL RECLAIM MY SLEEPING HOURS
(OR, I'LL NEVER SLEEP AGAIN)

With Buzz out of his crying phase, by the time he was one he had blossomed into an even happier child. He loved life, loved people and had turned into a complete entertainer – he's still like that now and absolutely loves making others laugh. You can see the utter delight on his face when he does something funny or skilful (like playing the drums) and gets a reaction.

There was one area, however, that caused us all a lot of continued distress.

Flipping bedtime!

When we got back from tour and things had settled down at home, we were still having to rock or cuddle him to sleep. At some point that turned into us putting him into his cot and sitting next to him on the floor – this was when he liked to hold one of our hands while he drifted off. It sounds adorable, but those irritating pinchers were out and looking for skin to nip. Eventually, once he realised pinching wasn't an option, things changed and we could sit in the rocking chair in his room, where he'd just look at us to make sure we were going to stay with him until he couldn't keep his eyes open any longer. This was better as at least it meant we could take our laptops up with us and get on with a bit of writing or replying to emails while we were being held hostage.

It was a really draining experience.

We knew he needed to sleep, we knew he'd sleep better if we weren't in there with him but he wouldn't let us leave, no matter how we conducted our escape. Don't get me wrong, sometimes we'd be out of there within a couple of minutes and it wouldn't be a big deal at all, but other times it would be more like forty-five minutes, or an hour – and then he'd catch me leaving (thanks to my cracking joints), meaning the process would have to start all over again.

He'd be a happy little chap when he woke up in the morning. Back to his usual self and full of smiles and babbling sounds. It was the hour in which he started calling for us that was the problem.

Five a.m.

FIVE A.M.

We'd groggily groan from under our duvet and look at the video monitor in disbelief, willing our ears and eyes to be wrong and begging our snoozy dreams not to stray too far. Nope. Too late. There he was, standing up and hanging on to the side of the cot, looking at his door and waiting for us to go in and get him. He'd always be so energetic and lively. We'd know instantly that that was it. Time to get up.

This is where we were naughty.

We'd put *The Muppets Take Manhattan* or *Frozen* on the TV and 'rest our eyes' while placing a hand on his leg or tummy, so that he couldn't crawl away from us, and let him laugh his way through his morning viewings of his favourite films while we got a little more much-needed shut-eye. In an ideal world the TV wouldn't go on until 6 a.m. Sometimes he'd come in to us at four o'clock and we'd be able to hug him back to sleep for a few more hours. Other times he'd come in at five and have no intention of doing anything of the sort, far too full of beans and eager for the day to start. He'd get ratty that Mummy and Daddy weren't being as enthusiastic as he was. Enter Kermit and Miss Piggy, or Anna and Elsa, whichever he was favouring more at the time.

Despite our appalling parenting skills, we'd always be downstairs by seven o'clock. That seemed a reasonable time to shake off the tiredness and take Buzz down for breakfast.

I know we weren't helping ourselves. I know we were giving him an incentive to wake up early and climb in with us, but in those moments when you're craving sleep because you've been up late the night before cramming in the work, you do whatever you can for an easy life. It never feels like the best time to start implementing new rules. I knew we were going to have to be firmer and stop rewarding unwanted behaviour, it was just a case of having the energy to do it in the morning when our brains hadn't had time to start functioning properly. Buzz could see we were weak, that our defences and our resolve weren't strong enough to fight against his infant charm.

I'd hear of other mums and dads having to drag their children out of bed at nine in the morning and breathe a little sigh of sorrow for all the sleeping hours I'd been missing out on. Why was my child so averse to letting us slumber on?

When Buzz was sixteen months old one friend told me

she'd introduced a Gro-clock and that it had dramatically changed their lives. This magical gadget basically uses images of suns and stars to communicate when it's time to go back to sleep and when to wake up. If a child wakes up and sees stars, they know to go back to sleep; if they see the sun, then it's time to wake up. Seeing as my friend's little boy was only a couple of weeks older than Buzz and he had completely grasped the concept, I decided we'd give it a go. In fact, I was on my Amazon app straight away and ordering it within seconds.

I needed to sleep.

I was so thrilled to see Buzz getting all excited as Tom showed him his new clock and talked him through the revised plan of how things were going to work in the mornings. I could feel my body practically melting with relaxation at the thought of a full eight hours of sleep . . .

Did it work?

Nope.

Not at all.

It took a full year for him to want to listen to what we had to say about that ruddy clock. Now it works like a charm!

Buzz currently gets up at 6.30, and I'm OK with that. Especially as he lies there in his big-boy bed (gosh, that transition was a total tear-jerker) waiting for the sun to do its thing on the clock before coming in to our room. He does the funniest things in that half-hour. He sings loudly, or acts out little scenes to himself – ones from programmes he's watched, or conversations he's heard. If I'm not deliriously tired still and wanting to make the most of the last few minutes of peace, I'll watch him. He's so amusing. And he's so excited when he comes running into our room shouting,

'Mummy, Daddy, I stayed in bed until the sun came up.' We both cheer him on, delighted at the happy start to the day, while waiting for his inevitable follow-up line – 'I done a poo in my pull-up.'

'Shotgun,' is our instant reply.

. . . . .

One thing I've realised with Buzz is that he prefers doing things in his own time – he understands what we're asking of him, he just doesn't necessarily want to do it. When it came to us leaving the room at night-time, it was him who finally instigated it. Tom was putting him to bed one night and he said, 'OK, Daddy. You go downstairs. Do some work.'

It was what we'd been trying to get him to let us do for months, but it came from him, as though it was his idea.

Tom said he was quite perplexed but did as instructed. We sat next to the monitor and watched Buzz, who simply rolled over and went to sleep. It was a blooming miracle!

Sadly it didn't last, thanks to a few changes that then occurred, like Buddy's arrival, Buzz starting nursery, and him discovering a new love of climbing.

I was putting his clothes into his wardrobe one day while he was playing next to me, and the next thing I knew he had his leg over the side of the cot and was scrambling to get into it. He landed face first on to the mattress. The joy of his own accomplishment was so apparent from his huge grin that getting a face full of mattress didn't register, or appear to cause any damage.

We instantly took the side off and transformed it into a toddler bed – it was fine him being adventurous and diving into the bed, but diving out of it would've resulted in him getting hurt. Now that he knew what he was capable of we didn't want him being tempted by a midnight break for freedom.

So we were back in the chair trying to get him to go to sleep and stopping him spending hours getting in and out of his bed simply because he could. Although now we could no longer sit there working as his little cheeky face would suddenly peep round the corner of the screen, the luxury of being able to get out of his bed not lost on him.

Actually his sleep became quite broken at this point, probably because he knew there was a major shift occurring. He'd get up in the night and want to come into our bed. But by this point Buddy had arrived and was sleeping soundly in his crib next to it, so there was no way we could risk Buzz coming in, being loud and waking him up, leaving us with two awake children at midnight. For this reason we started building another rod for our backs (why not? We all love creating habits we'll later have to break – parenthood would be too easy and completely boring without them): we started either taking him into the spare room (as mentioned in the introduction) or grabbing a pillow and blanket and sleeping on the floor next to him, so that he'd go back to sleep and not feel that we were neglecting him because of the new arrival. Sometimes he'd drift off straight away, and sometimes he'd decide if Mummy or Daddy was on the floor then that was exactly where he wanted to be. I learned to just sleep, rather than waiting for him to be fully asleep and then leaving. I'd wake up a little while later to him snoring in my face (one of the most beautiful things ever – I kid you not) and would gently put him back into his bed before removing my aching body (I'm already too old to be sleeping on the floor), climbing back into my bed, and getting some sleep before the next interruption came from either of them.

Occasionally they'd tag-team me – I'd finish feeding Buddy and would get into bed, then half an hour later Buzz would wake up and want me to sleep next to him. I'd comply and then have Tom waking me up a short while later because Buddy had woken up and needed a feed. Those were blurry nights that felt never-ending, but in hindsight, it didn't stay that way for long.

Things did calm down.

Then we moved Buzz into his big-boy bed in his spanking new bedroom.

As I've said above, that was a poignant moment. At least when he was in his cot with the side off it felt like he was still our baby, but the move put him into an actual bed – with a proper single duvet, and pillow.

The good thing about this move was that the bed had a roll-out trunk bed beneath it. We no longer had to sleep on the floor! Hurrah for our weary bones.

I've only slept on it a couple of times actually. Tom was usually the one to go in there to try and encourage Buzz back to sleep, but I don't think it's been pulled out for a couple of months now (how typical that now there's somewhere comfy to sleep, we're no longer needed). The difficulty was, once again, getting Buzz to go to sleep.

Enter another rod.

We started getting into his comfy bed with him and having a snuggle. Well, it was such a novelty to be able to fit into the bloody thing after trying to fit in the cot bed with him for so long – something that did end up happening on multiple occasions. His new bed was cosy, and I'm ashamed to say that

I sodding loved getting under his covers and having a little snooze before heading downstairs to get on with writing once he'd eventually fallen asleep.

We knew we were doing bad things. We knew it was going to come back to bite us in the arse . . .

We tried to backpedal pretty swiftly – sitting in the chair, or sitting on the floor . . . I was back to holding his hand and the whole thing taking quite a while.

It all changed in a big way when Tom was on tour with McFly and I was faced with a very testing few nights.

The night that caused it all to change started off normally with our usual bedtime routine of bath, bedtime stories and brushing teeth. It was lovely and fun, with us all happy and laughing. I then put Buddy down in his cot (so far he's pretty good at self-settling) and focused on Buzz. I gave him a big cuddle and helped him into bed. Straight away he asked me to get in. I explained that I wasn't going to get in but would sit on the floor next to him instead. He took it pretty well, and for a while I thought he was going to nod off fairly easily, but it didn't happen. Instead our sleep train, its journey already wobbly, completely derailed, with Buzz doing everything he could to put off the inevitable. He wanted the duvet on, the duvet off. He wanted water, he wanted some milk. He'd done a poo and needed his nappy changed. He wanted to hold my hand, he wanted me in the bed. He wanted his daddy . . . the list was endless. He was pulling out every single trick he could muster.

When I'd had enough of negotiating, and got a little firmer with him, that's when he started really sobbing my name, as though I was being the meanest mummy who ever walked the earth because I wanted him to go to sleep. Then everything intensified ten-fold thanks to him being overtired. He completely freaked out on me and started screaming. It was awful and even thinking about it now chokes me up. He was hysterical. It was so upsetting to see.

I ended up getting back into bed with him to try and calm him down, but even then he kept shouting in my face, 'Mamma, Mamma, Mamma.'

I held on to him so tightly, almost treating him like a baby as I tried to shush away whatever was going on in his head, but it didn't work. So I tried distracting him by talking about his day. Talking about things he'd been up to with Nanny and about the biscuits we'd made when he got home. He wasn't listening. The 'Mammas' kept coming.

They started to get quieter, as though he was saying them in his sleep. Several times he'd shut his eyes and would start gently snoring, but as soon as I moved to get out of the bed he would tug hold of my arm and start crying for me again, distraught at the idea that I might be leaving him alone in his bed – which seemed silly because he loves his bed so much. He was also pinching me throughout – and we're not talking little baby fingers grabbing away, but rather toddler hands that could inflict actual pain.

It all got too much for me and I ended up crying back at him, my face screwing up as the sobs I'd been trying to hold back shook their way out of my body. Buzz started laughing then, covering his face like I was and mimicking me – mistaking my tears for laughter. Thinking we were both in on the same joke.

I cried harder.

He stopped.

At some point I glanced at him again, and saw the sadness in his wide eyes as he looked at me, confused and sorry.

That look broke my heart. I shouldn't have been the reason for that sorrow.

Buzz fell quiet instantly, stopping crying as he closed his eyes, his little lips pursed. He was asleep within thirty seconds.

I knew he'd been playing me a little bit, that his tears had been put on at times, but I hadn't been able to do anything to stop him or snap him out of it. It was horrible seeing him so wound up. I was heartbroken that it had gone so far and had become so difficult for us both.

Buzz goes to bed at seven. That night I left his room at nine twenty-five and felt miserable. I came downstairs to my sister Giorgie and Chickpea and just cried my eyes out.

It was the worst night-time routine I've experienced with either of the boys to date (I seriously hope nothing ever comes along to top it).

To soothe my anguished heart I turned to social media. The response I got was overwhelming. Some people just gave me some much-needed support, while others detailed their own nights when they'd experienced something similar. I wasn't alone, and hearing that was the biggest comfort I could've received. I wasn't the only one being pushed. I wasn't the only one who felt like an absolute failure. I wasn't the only one struggling. It was amazing to share and to get comfort from a group of strangers whose support I truly needed and welcomed.

While I was busy in the realms of social media, Giorgie had been messaging one of her closest friends who she knew had been through something very similar and had called in a sleep expert to help. The friend helpfully passed on the knowledge that she'd picked up from the professional. It was essentially what I'd seen Super Nanny do time and time again, and it made perfect sense. I just had to put the new plan into action.

That night I bathed both the boys, read them stories – just like I do every night – while telling Buzz what was going to be happening when I put him to bed. Mummy was going downstairs to do some work, and he was going to stay in bed and go to sleep. He agreed. But as anyone with children knows, they might look like they completely understand what you mean and agree to comply, but when it actually comes down to doing what you've been talking about all day, the reality can be quite different.

After I brushed Buzz's teeth we walked into his room and said goodnight to the sun on his clock. I then knelt on his floor and gave him a huge hug, saying goodnight and confirming the plan for the night as I guided him into his bed and tucked him in.

At first he agreed again, but as I left and the door began to close the wailing started. I calmly said, 'Goodnight,' once more before heading to the stairs, ready to sit and watch the new plan unfold. I wasn't left sitting there for very long as Buzz ran out into the hallway, calling for me.

Very calmly, without saying anything or even looking at him, I took him by the hand and guided him back to bed. I didn't linger, or give him an extra hug.

More cries when I left.

He was back outside within seconds. 'Mumma, Mumma, Mumma.'

I repeated my earlier action.

He repeated his.

This went on for a good half an hour, with him wailing at me a few times to get into his bed, grabbing and pulling me.

I'd untangle myself and walk away.

You know the strangest thing, I didn't feel like a bad mum for doing so. I mean, obviously it's the worst thing in the world to hear your child crying for you and not go in to soothe them, but I felt like what I was doing was ultimately going to transform bedtime and make him much happier and more secure. So I stuck to my guns.

Eventually he stopped coming out of his room, deciding the tactic wasn't working, and instead sat on his bed and begged, 'Come in, Mumma. Come in.'

That was heartbreaking, but I was encouraged by the progress we'd made and didn't want to balls it up.

By quarter past eight Buzz was still sitting up, but he was rocking all over the shop. He was asleep, although whimpering my name every now and then when his rolling head would wake him up.

I did think about going in at that point, to help him just lie down so that he could get to sleep properly. I resisted my urges.

Fifteen minutes later he conceded and peacefully wriggled under the covers and went to sleep.

It was a major achievement! I know it still took an hour and a half, but I was happy knowing the plan had worked and was sure it would get easier each night once Buzz got used to it, and stopped relying on us being there.

Four hours later Buddy started wailing and woke Buzz up. With Tom away on tour I ended up saying Buzz could get into our bed with me. Well, one victory at a time is enough, plus it was lovely to just hold him after all the sobby cries at bedtime.

The next night Buzz only tried to come out of his room a

couple of times, and then started calling for Tom – well, if Mumma wasn't going to help him, then maybe Dadda would. He was asleep sitting up by quarter past seven, lying down and fully asleep by half past.

By the third night Buzz didn't try and come after me, or cry. He gave me a big hug, got into bed and rolled over to go to sleep.

We'd cracked it.

In that moment, a strange sadness settled over me that I hadn't been expecting. It was as though Buzz being able to happily settle himself put me out of a job, and had left behind a gaping emptiness. The truth is, a huge part of me loved being wanted and needed by my little boy, and this change symbolised him growing up. I wasn't sure I was ready for that yet.

· · · · ·

Tom couldn't believe the transformation that had occurred with our bedtime routine while he'd been away. He'd only been gone five nights but the change was so substantial that he was left a little awestruck at my work.

It makes such a huge difference to all of us if the boys go to bed when they're supposed to. First and foremost, they become well rested and happy, and then our working night can start at seven. Without the nightly struggle we're more focused and productive, meaning we get a lot more work done. The knock-on effect of that is that we don't spend the time we're with the boys thinking about the things we need to be getting on with when we aren't!

It's now lovely putting Buzz to bed. It's calm, loving and endearing. We cuddle while having a little chat about the day we've just had or the one that's coming, and then he climbs into bed, getting cosy under the covers with a little wiggle. It's so cute. He doesn't always go to sleep as soon as I leave. Sometimes he will lie there and chat to himself, or, as he does in the morning, he'll sing a few songs. Eventually that noise just stops, and he gives himself up to dreamland, the house becoming incredibly quiet – especially on a working night when there's no TV or radio on in the background.

I instantly look forward to the morning smiles we're going to receive from him 'when the sun comes up'. It might sound silly, but I do find myself missing my boys when they've gone to bed, even though I know they're just upstairs and that if they were to wake up it would be the start of our night-time plan derailing. What a catastrophe that would be! I think it's probably best to stay thankful for the peace and quiet and get on with my nightly 'to do' list.

· · · · ·

Usually things remain quiet when we go up to bed, but that doesn't last too long as I'm still up once or twice in the night with Buddy. You'd think I would learn and go to sleep at a reasonable time ready to grab whatever sleep I can, but that never happens.

The other night I must've fed him at least four times in the twelve hours I have dedicated to sleep in his 'baby diary' – he obviously can't read it. He's teething, he's had a cold, a cough. The list of exasperating variables is a never-ending one; there always seems to be something wanting to unsettle him and rob us both of our much-loved sleep.

Bizarrely, though, I don't seem to get stressed out any more about being up a few times in the night, or as passive-aggressive with Tom over the fact that I'm the one always having to get up because I'm the one with the babalons. Don't get me wrong, we have tried to change the habit (or remove the flipping rod).

We've had Tom go in there on numerous occasions, armed with his loving fatherly embrace and a bottle of water, but Buddy just screams his head off and becomes inconsolable. I wait for a while to see if he'll calm down, remembering what a midwife told me once about not giving in too easily – she said if babies know you'll come in after ten minutes they'll just keep going until you do. The problem is it's a blooming tough habit to crack when it's three in the morning and he's so distressed – it's like Buddy thinks he's literally never going to see me again, and it's difficult to listen to as it can't be nice for either him or Tom.

Inevitably, I go into the room.

As soon as Buddy sees me he leans forward and starts holding out his arms. As soon as I've taken him from Tom it's as though a switch has been flicked and he goes completely silent as he nuzzles himself into my chest, as though the last ten minutes haven't even occurred. Sometimes he even throws a sleepy grin at Tom, as if to say, 'This is all I wanted, Dadda.'

I think it's pretty upsetting for Tom for him not to be the needed one in that moment, but, on the plus side, it means he doesn't have to get up in the night, so I don't feel too bad for him. Ha!

Perhaps the reason I'm happy to just go with it and not get frustrated with the whole thing is because I know it won't last. Buddy will start sleeping through at some point, and he won't need those sleepy cuddles or his mother's comfort to help him do so.

The change will occur slowly; I might not even notice it at first as he starts waking later and later. But one morning I'll wake up and realise that I've woken of my accord and not because there's a baby crying or a toddler singing songs in the other room. I imagine I'll feel confused not to be startled awake. And then I imagine I'll panic and go check on them both.

· · · · ·

We currently have a fabulous night-time routine mapped out, which works whether we're here together or one of us is tackling them on our own. That being said, munchkins are unpredictable and it's best not to rest on your laurels or get smug about your achievements (and getting bedtime sorted is a big flipping achievement), because you can bet the moment you do things will get buggered up.

We're planning a big family holiday for next year where all four of us will be in the same room. Seeing as everything went tits up as a result of our trip to Australia, I am a little nervous (a lot. I am a lot nervous), but we still have to go on holiday and enjoy some dedicated family time. We have to live our lives and not be scared of a chaotic blip. However, I'm more aware than ever that I'll need to get back on their schedule as soon as we're back, in order to get rid of whatever 'rod' we might end up creating . . . wish us luck!

26
THE WAY TO A BOY'S HEART

THE WAY TO A BOY'S HEART

F ood is incredibly important in our house. It's something we all really enjoy and we are always talking about it. I would put it down to my Italian roots, but Tom is just as enthused as I am. We just love food – both the cooking and the eating of it. So I was really looking forward to introducing Buzz to solids. Unlike every other area of motherhood where I Googled and researched our options for hours and then spent forever pondering over the opinions of strangers, I knew straight away what I wanted to do when it came to giving Buzz food – and that was to give him *food*.

I'd seen 'BLW' written on Facebook a few times but had no idea what it meant. Luckily for us, our friends Cath and Greg were ready to enlighten us on the topic of baby-led weaning, as they'd used the method with their daughter Martha and raved (so hard they might as well have had glow sticks!) about how it had made her more adventurous with food and willing to try anything offered. It sounded fab. Even when

Greg was talking about choking, while screwing his face up and shaking his head as though it wasn't even an issue that the word had been uttered, I wasn't perturbed.

Hearing friends whose parenting skills we really respect and admire championing a technique they've successfully used, instantly piqued our interest.

There is so much conflicting advice out there when it comes to weaning a baby: giving baby rice from four months, putting rusks in their milk to bulk up the nutrients (one from my parents' generation), pureeing everything in sight, BLW, or a little bit of everything . . . and then there's the timing of it all – knowing when to start. So I liked the fact that I could decide not to listen to any of the confuddlement, and just follow Cath and Greg's recommendation.

I knew I wanted to do it, I just had to find out how, so I bought a book on the subject by Gill Rapley and Tracey Murkett, entitled *Baby-led Weaning* (genius) and devoured it quickly.

My understanding of BLW (which is a tiny bit different to the official definition, thanks to my baby brain, but encompasses all the main principles) is essentially that it allows your child to get to grips with food textures, colours and tastes through play. The play element means that at first they might not consume that much of what you've given them, but they're still getting all the goodness they need from milk, so that doesn't necessarily matter. BLW encourages them to be inquisitive and discover with their hands, as well as helping them figure out how to move lumps of food around their mouths and get the muscles working in there. So even when the dreaded gagging sounds occur, that's actually just a baby's mouth learning how to use certain muscles and finding their gag reflex, which is obviously what Greg had been talking about.

I discovered that the first important part of BLW is waiting until your child is ready, and not to be in too much of a rush.

Once Buzz was big enough to go into his high chair, we used to put him in it at our mealtimes, even if he wasn't ready to eat just yet himself, so he could see what we were up to and felt included.

At five and a half months Buzz had started to try and grab food off our plates. He'd gawp at us while we ate, his wide eyes following forkfuls of food from the dish to our mouths while his own mouth opened and closed, mimicking our chewing. His face would be filled with intrigue and confusion as to why he wasn't getting in on the action.

And he did want in on the action.

One day we were eating breakfast and decided to put a whole strawberry on Buzz's tray to see what he would do with it. Sure enough, within seconds he clamped his hand down on top of it with great force and then shoved it straight into his mouth, the red juice dripping down his chin as he bit into it. His face was a picture at the new cool sensation that was occurring in his mouth, as well as a taste that wasn't his mumma's milk.

He clearly loved its flavour as he didn't take his hand away from his mouth for ages, happily sucking the strawberry into oblivion.

Obviously I wasn't completely prepared for this monumental moment in his development as the lovely white babygro he was wearing turned bright red pretty quickly. In the coming weeks I realised it was time to ditch the white PJs I'd been using to enforce his bedtime routine, and buy clothes that wouldn't stain quite so much when food was smeared all over them. I did try and use bibs, but it was Buzz's sleeves that were the real problem as they used to end up dragging in everything – even when I rolled them up they found a way of landing in a pasta sauce or chicken curry.

For ease, sometimes I used to feed Buzz in only a nappy, but for the winter months I got some sleeved bibs that looked identical to the overalls children use in nursery when painting – they seemed to be the only way of keeping his clothes remotely clean. Plus his skin started getting irritated from being sticky, dirty, and then washed all the time.

AND THE MESS!

Gosh. BLW is messy! Very messy. Food goes everywhere

while they're exploring and have been given the freedom to do so, and I'm not just talking about over their clothes or in their hair. The kitchen floor and cupboards all got splattered in breakfasts, lunches and dinners in that first year.

Weetabix has to be the messiest cereal around, especially when smeared all over a baby's chair and in their hair, but both my boys have loved it so it's been a firm favourite at the breakfast table along with shredded wheat, melon, mango or bananas. Funnily enough, Buzz doesn't like strawberries any more. I'd say berries of any type are the only things he now refuses to eat.

Just like most first-time parents, I put a lot of thought and effort into the food I was giving Buzz. Obviously it all had to be nutritious, but for the first few weeks it also needed to be cut in a way he could handle with ease – chip-type fingers being the preferred shape. Butternut squash, sweet potato, broccoli, courgette, carrots, parsnips, asparagus, swede, baby sweetcorn – everything was either steamed, boiled or roasted to ensure it tasted good but also had a softer texture to it.

It cracked us up watching Buzz's face over the next few days, weeks and months as he discovered new flavours. He would always screw up his face as though he was sucking on a lemon, his body giving a little shudder as his empty hand bashed the table. At first we took the reaction to mean he didn't like what he was eating, but soon enough he'd hungrily go back for more, willing to give it a second, third and fourth chance.

It felt like Tom and I were on the journey with him and therefore it became something we could all get involved in and really enjoy. Mind you, in the early days our chosen method of introducing food freaked out all of our parents, who were used to the more conventional way of weaning using a spoon. They would fret over every solid bit of food going into his mouth. That being said, I can't blame my mum for feeling this way as she did witness Buzz gagging momentarily on a piece of cucumber in ASK Italian. I could understand her panic and confusion over why I was just watching him and giving him a few seconds to clear it. But he did and he was fine. My mum was in more of a tiz about it than he was, yet she grew to relax as she saw all the benefits of it – she even recommends BLW to other new parents now.

· · · · ·

For the first two years of Buzz's relationship with food, he had one great love: pasta.

He would've had pasta for breakfast, lunch, dinner and all the snacks in between if we'd let him. My sister Giorgie and I took Buzz to Sardinia to check out her wedding venue when he was fifteen months old. He was given a massive bowl of the stuff – it was literally the size of an adult's portion and he was in his element as he started tucking in. Ten minutes later a group of people came into the restaurant, took one look at Buzz and started laughing. His face was completely covered (and I really mean completely) with tomato sauce, and he had the biggest happy grin on his face. He was having the best time ever devouring that meal with his hands. The locals loved it, with one group even stopping to take photos of him – something I didn't mind in that situation.

With Buzz I tried to stick to BLW as much as possible. I liked putting a meal in front of him and leaving him to master it for himself. However, when we went for his eight-month review and mentioned BLW, the midwife shrugged her

shoulders and said, 'You can always do a bit of both,' and then carried on writing notes in Buzz's red book. (The book children are given at birth to record all their medical information, monitor their growth and chart their development.) It's ridiculous that the idea never crossed my mind – I'd been wondering how I was going to tackle yoghurts!

I've been a bit more chilled when it comes to Buddy and food. We've largely done baby-led weaning, but there were times early on where he would sit in his high chair not eating while looking at us hungrily. To encourage him a bit (I'm pretty sure this is going against all the BLW rules) I'd pop a bit onto a spoon for him. His legs and arms would start flailing around once he excitedly worked out what was happening. As soon as it was close enough, Buddy would grab the spoon and pull it into his face. It was clear he'd been watching all of us. He'd probably been wondering where his cutlery was.

Like his big brother, he loves pasta – although I've yet to see him make quite as much mess as Buzz used to. That said, Buzz might've made a lot of mess for a very long time, but it gradually got less and less, even more so when he worked out how to use a fork and spoon (we're still working on the knife).

The most annoying thing – which happened repeatedly, especially when they were first trying out all the new textures and flavours – was that you could guarantee the food that had taken the longest to prepare would be the dish to land on the floor mere seconds after it had been placed in front of either boy.

I quickly learned with Buzz to hand over smaller portions rather than handing it all over at once. It did help ease my heartache.

If I'd been really organised I'd have put a wipeable tablecloth underneath the high chair so I could keep putting the food back up on the tray . . . but I never got round to it. I didn't do it with Buddy, either, so I've clearly not learned anything. I could've just picked it up and given it back, I suppose, as

I don't live in the world's dirtiest house. Yet I don't really like doing the three-second rule with the boys. Instead those discarded bits usually find their way into my mouth – sometimes even the soggy, slightly questionable bits.

I can't believe I've just admitted that . . . Although do calories really count if the food in question was picked up off the floor after being intended for a clumsy minor?

I think this one is up for debate.

. . . . .

I do appreciate that BLW isn't for everyone on account of the mess, and the fact that a baby smeared with food can be a horrifying sight for those who aren't used to food being introduced in that way, or if you are particularly attached to having a clean house, but we've just gone with it and love seeing our little boys enjoying mealtimes at the dinner table with us all eating the same thing. I have to pinch myself sometimes when we're all sitting around like that, eating together in a civilised way. It's in those moments that it really dawns on me that I have a family, and that I'm fulfilling my OXO mum dream from years ago. It's a pretty cool realisation to have.

Obviously there have been a few challenges along the way too.

When Buzz was still in his high chair we rarely struggled to get him to eat his food. In fact, we'd always know he was ill if he wasn't fussed by it – if he refused a plate of pasta we knew it was serious. The difficulties came when he was taken out of his high chair (Buddy is now in it) and started experiencing the novelty of freedom at mealtimes. Being able to get up and walk is very tempting when you know you can.

As a result we've had to (and occasionally still have to) persuade him to sit back in his chair to stop him running in circles around the dinner table (especially if he's finished and we're still going). Repeatedly telling a toddler to sit back down and having to enforce some sort of discipline at a time that should be jolly, relaxed and a real occasion of togetherness, really does suck!

He still has a very healthy appetite, though, and regularly asks to try something we're eating if he's not been given the same thing. 'Mine try it' seems to be a catchphrase of his right now – even if he's just after Aunty Giorgie's toast, which he certainly doesn't need to 'try' to see if he likes it. He knows perfectly well what it is, and that it's 'delicious'. He just knows we like him trying things, so cheekily used that to his advantage!

27
WHAT GOES IN MUST COME OUT –
IDEALLY ON THE TOILET!

WHAT GOES IN MUST COME OUT – IDEALLY ON THE TOILET!

don't think a book detailing my experiences of being a mum would be complete without a bit of poop chat. Weirdly, it's become one of my favourite topics over the last three years. I developed an obsession with seeing the newborn poop changing from black to its curry-like state, always breathing a sigh of relief that it wasn't too green and still contained those little lumpy bits (I'd read somewhere they were good). I still can't change a poopy nappy without feeling the need to give some internal commentary about the sight I've been greeted with.

Sadly some great love stories must come to an end. At some point I had to surrender my interest in the contents of Buzz's nappies and let the toilet gobble them up instead.

How to go about making that change was the daunting bit.

Buzz was about eight months old when a friend from school messaged me on Facebook to tell me of a method she'd been using with her daughter since she was six months old, whereby she'd put her on the potty throughout the day. Her own mum had told her that it was very common for children to be potty trained very early back when my friend and I were younger, because of all the faff with washing nappies (in those days disposables were only just becoming available) – parents wanted their children out of them as soon as possible!

Apparently my friend's daughter was amazing at going on the potty from the get-go, achieving a wee on her first visit and a poop on her second. That was pretty impressive and I salute my friend for having the patience to carry on with this method – by the time we spoke about it her daughter was seven months in and my friend could count on one hand the number of times her daughter had pooed in her nappy during that whole period. Incredible!

I did start looking into it, but I just felt it wasn't for me. Plus, now that I was back at my desk and writing, I didn't want to have to pass that responsibility on to my mother-in-law or my parents.

· · · · ·

'Is he out of nappies yet?' has been a common question we've faced since Buzz was only about fourteen months old. It seems I'm not the only one obsessed with poop. It's a universal thing.

The inquisitive nature of others has added some pressure, as it's made me constantly worry if I should be worried. I know – worrying about worrying! It sounds crazy, but I've come to terms with the fact that a huge part of being a mother is accepting that it's my duty to worry about all things concerning my boys, no matter how trivial they might seem to others.

Interestingly, Buzz has never been fussed about having a

wet or dirty nappy. He'd happily keep playing away while acting oblivious to the nappy swinging between his knees (I never let it go that far, but it was fun to write). So how could I get a boy who didn't care about this to start caring? It was something to ponder.

At some point we bought a couple of potties, to see which one he liked, and to entice him in to our little plan. However, Buzz wasn't particularly bothered by them. He'd play with them every now and then – he'd tip them over or bash them around a bit, sometimes wearing one as a hat – but he'd never really sit on them. Actually we had tempted/bribed him into doing a poo on his potty once because he wanted to watch a random video of Harry Judd giving a speech on his birthday, but that was the one and only time it had happened before we started proper potty training. We thought we'd cracked it, but it was most definitely a fluke – or it goes to show just how much our little man loves Harry!

When Buzz turned two years old Huggies had got in touch and asked if I'd work with them. They wanted me to produce a video for my YouTube channel that detailed our potty-training experience. As I knew I'd be talking about it on there anyway, and really respect Huggies as a brand, I agreed to do it. There was no time pressure, we could take as long as we needed to get going, and the team there were incredibly supportive and gave amazing advice from a potty-training guide they'd been working on with an expert. I obviously listened to what they were saying, but at the same time I simply wanted Buzz to be on the loo, achieving what so many people had asked me about. Everyone else had made it seem like it was so easy . . .

By the time I agreed to work with Huggies, Buzz was two

and four months. He was incredibly bright and switched on, he could follow instructions and really communicate. I thought we were good to go. I felt he was ready.

A big box of goodies arrived from the brand – pull-ups, stickers, big-boy pants, charts, soap, PJs – extra little treats to help us kick off our journey. However, even while I was going through it all, Buzz was more engrossed in the box it came in, and was busy playing hide-and-seek. That should've been a warning sign about how interested and ready he was to give the contents of the box a go. He wasn't.

I had a flick through the guide that had been sent over and spotted a little tick chart for parents to complete to see if their child was ready to start potty training. I was dubious when I read about signs like your child asking to be changed, asking to use the potty or asking to use underwear (Buzz had asked about none of these things); however I was encouraged by the fact he could follow instructions, pull his trousers up and down and stay dry for two hours.

I felt Buzz could master the skill of using the loo!

It was all quite exciting at first when we took off his nappy and put on some big-boy pants, explaining that if he needed to go to the toilet he could go on the potty. He nodded at us and verbally responded in a way that made it seem he was one hundred per cent with us on our mission.

Two minutes later he weed on the floor, looking at the puddle by his feet before turning to me and saying, 'Uh-oh. Mess, Mumma.'

We kept calm as we reminded him about the potty, popped him in new pants and went again.

Same thing happened.

Then again.

And again.

Within the first hour we had heard 'Uh-oh, mess' four times, with Buzz looking surprised and bewildered each time about why his feet were suddenly wet.

We were chilled out in our approach, but we found it incredibly frustrating by the end of the day when Buzz refused to go onto the potty and kept wetting his pants with the same look of confusion on his face.

It didn't get better the next day, either. Instead we had lots of tears and tantrums as Buzz struggled to get to grips with what we were asking him to do.

At the start of the third day Buzz sat on the potty with his pants on, saying he needed a wee. We cheered at his achievement and then tried to get him to take down his pants before he wet them again. This led to an almighty meltdown and to him boycotting the potty altogether. He'd scream and cry when we suggested he sit on it, wrestling his way out of our arms if we tried to encourage him on there. I actually don't think I've seen him sit on one since.

I wish we'd have left him on the potty in his pants, as I've since discovered that doing that is all part of learning – the important thing was just that he was on there – but I didn't. Having said that, there's no point beating myself up over it, as I suspect we'd have come to the same conclusion we eventually did, anyway. It was clear we weren't the only ones frustrated by the task and it was all just too overwhelming for him. He became incredibly anxious and it was clear he was holding in his number twos.

Potty training wasn't fun.

I hated seeing him so distressed, so we aborted mission. Quite frankly, it wasn't worth him getting into such a state over it when he clearly wasn't ready. He visibly relaxed the second we put his nappy back on, although still freaked out if he was anywhere near the potty or his big-boy pants.

Some people will probably say we should've persevered with it, but it was too much. We know our child and we knew that nothing good would've come from a sterner approach.

I felt awful. I'd read the whole situation incorrectly and had rushed even though I'd been told not to. I'd wanted to get on with it and had been too eager, therefore I found myself focussing on the end goal when I should've been looking at the smaller steps that came before it.

Hindsight, my friends, is bloody great but extremely un-useful.

It seems I'm not on my own in this department as I've spoken to lots of mums, especially mums of boys, who've found themselves in exactly the same situation when they've tried potty training around that age. Hearing comforting words from other mums made me realise, once again, that all children are different and develop at different rates and at different times.

Buzz was busy learning how to master the drums and jump around with his guitar. No wonder he wasn't too fussed about sussing out how to pee in what was, essentially, a plastic bucket. It wasn't much fun in comparison.

· · · · ·

I didn't dare talk about potty training with Buzz for a couple of months after that, and I certainly didn't suggest he went on the potty or wore big-boy pants. No way! I didn't want the nightmare experience to become an even bigger issue in Buzz's mind. If I'm totally honest I was hoping he'd completely forget about the whole thing, that the episode could be erased from his memory entirely.

Eventually I stumbled across a book on the internet called *Pirate Pete's Potty*, which had fab reviews. I bought it and just left it in Buzz's room. One night he picked up the book and wanted to read it – it has an enticing sound button, so I'd been hoping this would happen. We read it together and he cackled his way through, joining in with the narrative and choosing a potty and pair of big-boy pants from the ones illustrated – he went for the red frilly ones adorned with hearts because they tallied with his admiration for Lightning McQueen and anything red. He's stayed loyal to that pair of frillies ever since.

He thoroughly enjoyed listening to Pirate Pete's account of potty training, the little cogs in his head clearly turning as he processed what was going on. Still, we didn't push him but were thankful he was interested and that we hadn't ballsed it up completely.

We also started taking him to the bathroom with us, so that he was more aware of what happened in there.

I think one of the only negatives of both Tom and me being around more while writing from home was that Buzz hadn't been coming on loo trips with us as there was always someone else around to take care of him. He wasn't seeing what was happening in there, so we made an effort to ensure that the purpose of the toilet seat became more apparent. Although with that came the observation that Mumma doesn't have a willy-winkle like Dadda and Buddy. Hearing 'Mumma's willy-winkle's gone' really did make me chuckle.

One day, two months after we'd started and failed our potty-training mission, Buzz was running around the house playing with a crash helmet on (as you do). Suddenly he stopped what he was doing, went to the downstairs loo and shouted, 'I need the toilet!' We dropped everything and ran to join him, excitedly whipping off his trousers and nappy before placing him on the toilet seat. He laughed before a look of absolute concentration took over his face, a look that softened into delight and pride.

He blooming well did it!

Buzz peed on the toilet!

I managed to grab a picture of Buzz, sitting on the loo wearing his bright green crash helmet, giving a big thumbs-up to the camera at his achievement. It's such an adorable photo, but I think it'll be one to embarrass him with when he's older – as you can imagine, it was incredibly funny.

Obviously the journey didn't end there (I wish it had), but this time round I had no doubt that Buzz was ready, interested and excited. More importantly, though, I was willing to take things as slowly as he needed me to.

We're currently two months in to getting Buzz 'dry'. He's very good at going to the toilet for a wee, but is still reluctant to do a number two in there. Instead he prefers to wait until he has a pull-up on at either naptime or bedtime and goes then – which is pretty clever of him, really, but not quite what we're after.

I know he'll get there, though, so I'm not too concerned. Nor do I want to try forcing him into doing something he's uncomfortable with. Things just click with Buzz and then he's extremely happy to go along with his own discoveries. We just have to sit and wait for that to happen.

· · · · ·

I've actually got a new obsession to replace my poo one – big-boy pants. My sister was staying with us while we started to potty train Buzz and found it hysterical that almost every delivery that arrived at our house was another selection of pants (multi-coloured, Mickey Mouse, *Cars* or *In the Night Garden*). I can't help myself. I find them incredibly sweet.

I think Buzz has more underwear than I do right now.

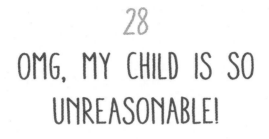

28
OMG, MY CHILD IS SO
UNREASONABLE!

OMG, MY CHILD IS SO UNREASONABLE!

I watched the Pixar film *Inside Out* when Buzz was one and a half. Although at the time I felt lucky that Buzz was such a level-headed, reasonable human being who was obedient and thoughtful, I had an inkling that it might not stay that way for long. Not that those character traits would leave him and that he'd totally change, but that the emotions unleashed by imminent new developmental stages would lead to some testing parenting moments. There had to be some truth in the terms 'terrible twos' and 'threenager' – behaviour phases I'd been hearing about for years. In my pre-mummy days I'd always thought people were exaggerating about this specific stage, but I feared it nonetheless.

I found myself on high alert, waiting for the meltdowns and getting prepared for whatever was to come our way – slightly squinty in suspense whenever Buzz showed reluctance to be rational and wondering whether we were about to witness an uprising: the start of him campaigning for toddler rights on behalf of all mini-humans everywhere.

Is this it? I'd think to myself whenever there was a wobble, only to breathe a sigh of relief when the situation was easily deffused seconds later thanks to a little distraction.

I fear I've lulled you into a false sense of contentment with the last part of the previous sentence, because the tantrums did come. It's just that they seemed to build over time, the causes becoming less predictable, increasingly trivial and more offensive. Our crimes against him worsened as time went on. How dare we ask him to put his socks on, not let him drive our car to nursery, give him the dinner he asked for, or stop him from playing the drums during a McFly soundcheck when he was clearly their new drummer! How could we be so insensitive as to ask him to put a coat on so that he didn't get cold in the snow, stop him from playing with scissors or not let him put his dirty (poo-filled) nappy back on?

Why were *we*, his parents, being so difficult? So unyielding? Since when had *we* become so unsupportive and annoying? Honestly, it's a wonder he managed to put up with us.

We were idiots.

Clearly.

When the struggles and outbursts did occur, I found myself thinking back to *Inside Out* and imagining all the little emotions in his head at war with each other and chucking out balls of feelings willy-nilly, causing an absurd theatrical display of gargantuan size.

Thinking of his irrational behaviour in this way made me understand the chaos a little more. It made me realise my darling boy wasn't really to blame for his outbursts; rather, he was simply learning how to process his emotions and deal with life!

The majority of the time there seems to be no rhyme or reason, no logic or rationale behind his mood swings – and that's not the easiest thing to deal with. Sometimes I find myself staring at him when he's gone into full-on meltdown mode, my jaw on the ground, wondering what on earth I should do to calm down this child who seems to have become possessed. I try to divert his attention away from whatever it is he's lost his cool over. Sometimes that makes it worse. I try to talk to him in hushed, caring tones about what he's feeling. Sometimes that makes it worse. I try to be firmer. That always makes it far worse. Sometimes I do nothing. That can still make it worse.

Sometimes it feels like nothing works, with everything I try being of no avail.

I can't even tell you how I get him to stop and snap out of it, because there is no one method. Each episode is entirely unique, and terrifying for that reason. I pick my way through as though I'm in a minefield, treading carefully to avoid making the situation blow up further.

Eventually he just stops and clicks back into the sweet and loving mummy's boy that I know him to be. It's such a sudden switch, the speed at which it happens always making my head spin.

I breathe a sigh of relief, my heart instantly softening and moving forward with him, not wanting to focus on the absurdity of what has (or hasn't) happened. I'm an adult, I know there's no point harping on and rehashing a bad situation. I don't need an apology in that moment or for him to regret 'acting up'. Him moving on from it is everything I could possibly need.

I know he's still learning.

He's only two and eight months, so we have a long way to go until we're in the clear, guys. I heard on the radio the other day that boys become more agreeable at seven years old, but that it all goes to shit again when they're eleven . . . That's not a very big window of level-headed thinking. However, someone else's experiences aren't mine. I'd rather figure all that out for myself.

. . . . .

I find it harder to deal with the terrible twos when we're out in public, because then I'm not simply dealing with the two of us, but also wondering who's watching and judging me for my handling of whatever situation has occurred, something that affects my ability to navigate myself around the drama unfolding.

There's a lot of deep breathing and occasional bribery while I try and divert his fickle emotions towards something else. 'Come on, let's go home and make biscuits' is always a good one. An urge comes over me to get us moving, away from the scene of the crime, into the car and home to our safe haven.

I can remember being really told off when I was younger and we were out in public – Mum had a special way of hissing at us through her teeth, a warning to 'pack it in'; if it became more than that, if she raised her voice at us and let rip, then we knew we were in serious trouble and would fall silent instantly. I can't imagine how difficult it must've been to drag the three of us around the shops – especially as she didn't drive back then so we used to have to get the bus everywhere. It's little realisations like that that give me a whole newfound respect for my mum. I honestly don't know how she did it. The three of us never made it easy for her as we used to fight loads, too. It was a combination of our feisty Italian side and a bit of Essex 'balls'. We were a handful.

I've only just started to get more comfortable with taking both Buzz and Buddy out together. Until now I've been doing the majority of the shopping I need online. Actually, I'm still doing that – gosh, I don't know how Mum coped without the world of online shopping. She had to do literally all her shopping traipsing around the high street with us in tow. Jeeeeez!

I didn't take the boys out on my own at first because I was recovering and it would've been too much, and after that Tom was around most of the time so I never really had to fly solo. Months went by without me having to take them out on my own, and so when the time came for me to do so it was a daunting prospect.

It's a lot like learning to ride a bike – the more you do it, the easier it is. OK, that analogy doesn't quite work. Bear with me. Sometimes you fall off it, and then your world turns upside down for a moment or two in the process. Then you get up, get back on the bike and keep focusing forwards. Sometimes the whole of motherhood is like that, not just the 'going out in public with your adored offspring' bit.

I probably shouldn't write this as I know it'll come back to bite me on the arse, but I don't think Buzz has ever really had a full-on meltdown in public. He's misbehaved and pushed my buttons, of course, but from memory (and mine isn't the most reliable thing ever) that's as far as it's gone. Tom did take a photo of him once face down on the floor in a card shop, refusing to budge, but I think that's as extreme as it's got . . . perhaps I just don't take him out enough.

His cheekiness has increased at home, though, and there's no denying it feels as though he's doing certain things to test out his boundaries and see how far he can push us without being told off.

A few months ago I went all Super Nanny on him and introduced the 'naughty step'. That changed things dramatically, and showed him there were consequences for doing things we'd asked him not to – things that were usually for safety reasons, like jumping on the sofa, throwing things or being too heavy-handed with Buddy.

You could always tell he agreed with the decision to place him on the step by the speed in which he ran there. It was horrible seeing him on it – he'd always (fake) cry, saying, 'Mummy, I get off now. Mumma, I want to get off now' – but I'd leave him there for two minutes and wouldn't talk to him so he would understand it was serious and not a game.

It was going really well, but I didn't like it when he started saying, 'Buzz is naughty.' I didn't want him to label himself in that way, but rather understand that some *actions* are naughty, so instead we renamed it the 'time out' step – a spot to sit and reflect on what's just happened and to show a little remorse.

I leave him on there for two minutes before going over and sitting in front of him. I then ask him why he was sent to the step, to see if he's understood. More often than not right now he'll respond, 'I bashed Buddy,' even if he hasn't, but he knows that's the one we get most upset about. He's usually so lovely with him, but every now and then he'll push him, snatch a toy off him, or, now that Buddy's on his feet, peel his hands off whatever it is he's using for balance and give his chest a little nudge. This always results in Buddy falling over and bashing his head, and therefore it's the only offence at which I will bellow (yes, I am capable), 'Buzz. Time out step. Now!'

He basically sprints there while I check if Buddy is OK.

Once we've had a little chat about why he was sent there, he apologises to me (and Buddy if he was involved), saying, 'I'm sorry, Mumma, I won't do it again. I'm sorry, Buddy, I won't do it again,' in the sweetest way possible, as though his heart really is filled with the best of intentions. I know it's just a case of all those emotions running wild inside him, giving him the sudden urge to lash out, or be more boisterous and chaotic, so I'm never really mad at him. It's just my role as his parent to show him right from wrong, and to start teaching him that there are consequences to some actions.

With the apologies over he then stands up and gives me a cuddle. I can't help but love him a little more when he hugs me in that calm moment, before he runs off and starts playing again, ready to cause more mayhem. I love feeling just how unconditional the love I have for him is – and his for me.

· · • · ·

There are also simpler daily struggles that we require no 'step' for, yet I still sometimes need considerable negotiating skills in order to persuade Buzz to comply. Getting him to complete tasks like putting his shoes on, brushing his teeth or getting into his car seat can all require every ounce of strength and patience I have. I'm not even talking anything physical, although I have had many a laughing wrestle with Buzz while trying to do something as simple as get a toothbrush into his mouth. We end up both getting the giggles.

Tom actually did something I was surprised at with regard to getting Buzz to willingly brush his teeth, and that was show him pictures of black, decayed teeth – the sort you might see when sitting in the waiting room at the dentist's. It was a bold move, but he seems to understand now that serious consequences come with not letting Mummy and Daddy brush his teeth properly. Don't get me wrong, he still tries it on sometimes, but it's a lot better. Buddy has just started brushing his two teeth (so cute) at the same time, so it's more fun at the moment anyway. They both giggle their way through it.

It's fun and games, this parenting malarkey.

29
WHAT'S IT LIKE WITH TWO?

WHAT'S IT LIKE WITH TWO?

I often get asked 'What's it like with two?' Sometimes I don't get a chance to reply before the enquirer chips in with 'I bet it's manic', so I just go along with their answer with a laugh and a nod. Parenthood has robbed me of the ability to sit and reflect on how we're finding it all. It's ever-changing, ever-evolving – hour by hour, minute by minute – it shifts. I could answer a million different ways in one twenty-four-hour period if some plonker asked me on repeat.

Before Buddy arrived I'd look at Buzz, so full of energy and drive, and wonder what it was going to be like to add another little person into the mix. Having said that, I did want him to have a sibling, a playmate to dream alongside and let his imagination run wild with. When Buzz turned nine months I was hit with the realisation that if I were to fall pregnant at that very moment, there'd be eighteen months between my two children. It seemed absolutely crazy to be thinking about having another when Buzz was still so small, but I know loads of people who have that age gap with their siblings – it's not that uncommon. Plus, it might have sounded scary at the time, but it's not as though I was going to drop a baby there and then – Buzz would still have had an extra nine months of development and growth before his sibling arrived on the scene. All the same, I wasn't ready – mentally, physically or book-wise. I'd been signed for novels three and four, and didn't want to feel I was rushing to fit in the birth of a baby.

So having carefully considered the issue and weighed everything up, I decided I'd quite like two years between child one and two. This was heavily influenced by something I'd read about an older sibling being more accepting if the newborn arrived within a certain time period. I've since learned not to believe everything you read and to instead focus on the individuality of each child rather than make sweeping generalisations, but it definitely played on my mind.

Before we knew it we'd come to the time where we'd have to start 'not, not trying' to achieve a two-year age gap. We spoke about it briefly. I fell pregnant that month. Yes, it was that simple. I couldn't quite believe it. I was one of the annoying ones who might as well have got impregnated with just a saucy look. It happened so fast and for that reason it was all a little surreal.

I didn't feel bad for Buzz that his time with us was going to be shared with another human. I didn't have a sense of guilt about it. I know it's something that many mums and dads admit to feeling – I mean, I did hold him tightly every now and then, knowing he was no longer going to be the only one I loved unconditionally, or the most dependent one in the house, but I didn't feel anything more than that. Nothing unbearable or heart-wrenching. I was excited for him – excited for all of us. It was a happy time, and the effect of his sibling's arrival on Buzz wasn't something I particularly worried about. This was helped by the fact Buzz loved my bump. He'd stroke and kiss it, saying, 'Hello, baby.' It was adorable.

But yes, how was I going to cope having two children under two in the house?

When we first brought Buddy home I was struck by how calm everything was. We'd been there before so felt like we knew what we were doing. We were confident in our approach but laid-back in our delivery.

We didn't faff as much, and made sure we got to enjoy time with just the four of us. Funnily enough, the visitors were far fewer this time around. Not that we were complaining. It gave us time to adjust to the new family dynamic, and for Buzz to get to grips with the fact he had a little brother.

During the first week of us being home, the mornings would always start the same, with Buzz getting into our bed and holding Buddy. The delight and awe on his face spoke volumes. He was in love, and his love made my heart melt.

Buzz had suddenly become more capable and easier to deal with, possibly deciding to take his big brother role very ser-iously, and Buddy was a fab little newborn who loved sleeping – he'd even sleep through Buzz playing the drums. They were the perfect pairing.

So back then, when people used to ask me, 'How is it with two?' I used to say that it was calmer than having just the one. It was!

But as time goes on, each of the children move into new phases; they hit new milestones, new hurdles and obstacles, they learn new skills and celebrate new successes, and it's because things are forever moving and unfolding that I now find it difficult to answer that question. Just when you think you've got the lie of the land, the youngest one will start rolling over, or the oldest will start stringing longer sentences together and need even more from you as he practises his new under-standing of the English language. The youngest will start walking, or the oldest with be ducking his way through potty training. There's always so much to process, so much to think about at any one time. We are forever adapting.

Motherhood isn't a fixed thing. It's moving and free-flowing, set to change at any given moment. You can't afford to get comfy and feel like you've got it all down. Well, I say that, but if you *are* feeling like you're on top of things then maybe you should enjoy that feeling while it lasts – because in an hour your two-year-old is going to develop an obsession for his scooter (that he hasn't used since you bought it for him), and you're going to have to learn how to juggle a newborn in a carrier, a scooter and a toddler when he ultimately stops wheeling himself around on your family walk and insists on being carried instead (yes, this has happened).

I can remember Tom and me chatting to a stranger in a lift in Melbourne. She saw Buzz and had the biggest grin on her face. After we'd talked for a little while, we found out she had two children. She said something along the lines of, 'You think you love him now, but wait until he has a sibling. Seeing them together, seeing them interact, love and care for each other is the best feeling in the world.'

Now I understand what she was saying. At the end of today's naptime I heard Buzz calling me upstairs. He wasn't in his bed in his room as I'd expected. Instead he was on the floor in Buddy's room, sitting in front of his cot and making him laugh.

How is life with two? It's flipping knackering, manic and chaotic. I can only imagine what it's going to be like when Buddy can give back a little and manages to stick up for himself.

Yet the sight of them together, witnessing the sparkle in their eyes as they make each other cackle with laughter at whatever nonsense they're dreaming up, is so incredibly heartwarming.

It's magical, and the biggest reward I think I'll ever receive.

It's what makes me hope for and look forward to having more children.

Yes, I did just write that – I want to be the OXO mum, remember?

I haven't spent much time thinking about the jump from two to three children, as we've only just made the step from one to two, but whenever the subject arises (it always does in interviews) I get asked if I'd go for a third 'to get the girl'.

No.

Gender doesn't bother me, so that really wouldn't influence my decision about whether or not to have another child. I wish for a healthy baby, not someone to put in pink dresses – not that I think I would go down the pink route, but who knows. I am partial to a bit of floral, so that would be lovely . . .

Funnily enough, having had two boys, the arrival of a girl would throw me completely. I think I'd feel like I was a newbie again. Saying that, I'm a little more clued up with girls now that my sister has had Summer Rae. It's not quite as daunting as it could've been.

Anyway, with so much going on I doubt we'll be making the jump to having three (or four) children for a couple of years or so. I know there's no such thing as perfect timing and that you can only plan to a certain extent before nature takes over, but I would love for things to be calmer before I fall pregnant again.

But in the end, what will be will be, and I'm already thankful to my two little rays of sunshine for arriving here safely. I already feel content.

30
LEARNING TO JUGGLE

LEARNING TO JUGGLE

If I'm honest I don't think I've quite got the mum/work balance right at this precise moment in time. Or maybe I'm just realising that I'm going to have to constantly adapt my juggling technique to feel like I've got everything under control for even short bursts of time.

As the boys grow, what they need from me is changing. As my career progresses, the demands alter. At times I feel like a puzzle-owning ninja, trying to swiftly slot together millions of pieces to create a seamless image, rather than one that's disjointed and full of holes.

It's not just my books, there's the vlogging, blogging, writing columns, television-presenting and plenty of Facebook Live chats – they all require my attention, focused mind and, of course, time. Time is one thing that seems to disappear as soon as I'm blessed with some; that lazy spare morning or that rare night off seems like a long-forgotten dream. Gone in a flash. All the put-off chores suck time up too, though at least doing them is a positive use of time – because everything needs to get done, and sometimes putting things off just adds to the pressure of it all. Right now my 'to do' list seems never-ending.

One thing I'm asked time and time again is how I juggle. The idea that people think I've discovered some secret formula to getting shit done makes me chuckle – both with humour and with nervousness. The truth is, I haven't. When projects come up that I like the sound of, even though I know they're going to require my time (of which I have none), I seem inclined to take on the opportunity and think later. In fact, it seems I usually drop my balls when I look up and start realising how many of them I've got in the air – as though I'm suddenly made aware of the almighty feat ahead of me and I realise that I'm crackers for even attempting it.

I'm far better at focusing on what's in front of me and calmly getting tasks ticked off my list, something that's becoming more manageable now I've got organised. This doesn't involve anything fancy, I just have a hand-drawn three-month calendar on my office wall, alongside a list of projects which tells me how much I have left to do for each one. Each project has a series of empty squares attached to it – if I film a video, a box gets ticked. If I edit that video, a box gets ticked. If I upload that video . . . I think you get the point. I thoroughly enjoy ticking a box. I love the feeling of relief that comes with getting stuff done. It's quite addictive, almost euphoric – OK, that's possibly a tad over the top, but I just love completing tasks!

Mind you, I don't always stay on top of it all – I miss vlog uploads, Facebook Live chats (I'm currently meant to do every Tuesday evening and Thursday morning) and the occasional blog. The little square on my wall stays bleakly blank – actually, I then circle it with a Sharpie pen, to make sure I know I've not done it. That way I ensure I don't miss two of anything in a row . . . well, in an ideal situation, anyway.

So no, I don't get everything done, but largely I am managing it all right now because at this point in time I know people are asking more of me than ever before, but that might not last forever. In fact, it's highly likely it won't. So, for the sake of my family's future I need to be running with it while I can. I've become a 'yes' woman, eager to see what's going to pop up next and where it'll take me.

Family is always my top priority, though, and I wouldn't do anything I think could be detrimental to my life with Tom and the boys. They are my core. They are the reason for everything that I do. They are my home. My heart.

When I was growing up, my mum was in charge of us three children and running the house. Dad went out to work, some-times seven days a week, in the hope of providing us with a comfortable life. Dad and his siblings didn't have much when they were growing up in the small village of Valva in Italy, so he wanted to ensure we did have nice things, even if it meant him working all the time. Sadly, when that sought-after comfortable life had been achieved my mum and dad got divorced. It wasn't the best time of our lives, but we're all fine with it now. My mum and dad are more than comfortable being around each other and would even class themselves as friends – something that really confuses people when we're all out together and they're with their new other halves (I say 'new', but Dad's been with the lovely Debbie for nearly a decade). We are all relaxed and happy with our unconventional family set-up, but it does remind me how important it is to have a balance when it comes to working hard and enjoying life as a family.

I had an extremely happy childhood (minus the bullying at school) – and that was solely down to my wonderful family. My Italian heritage means I've always placed an emphasis on the importance of love and respect within the home, and I love and respect both my mum and my dad and really admire them for the choices they made in bringing us kids up! I think you write down the word 'divorce' and people instantly conjure up a miserable image of parents at loggerheads and children being pulled in both directions – luckily for us that wasn't, and isn't, the case.

As time with the family is of utmost importance, I try to make sure both Tom and I have weekends off, as well as one day in the week if we're not both working towards a deadline or really struggling to get everything done (sadly this happens more often than I'd like to admit).

That free day in the week feels entirely different to the weekends. There's something extremely calming about being off together as a family in the week when a large proportion of the population is either at work or in school. You don't have the chaos of the weekends where everything is, invariably, much busier, with everyone trying to cram in time at the park or at the shops, doing anything to get their minds off work.

A further incentive for having that midweek slot of family time is knowing we won't be able to have it forever. The boys will both be at school before we know it and then our time together will be limited to weekends and school holidays. I can't even think about schools right now without getting teary. Why do they have to grow up? WHY? It just seems so unfair.

I try and work four days a week, but then I pick up my work again in the evenings, too. Those few hours of working without disruptive emails pinging through is becoming increasingly invaluable. Now that the children are finally going down to sleep at seven it means that by one minute past the hour we are downstairs and cracking the whip. Occasionally we're up until midnight, only stopping because one of us will mention heading up to bed – reminding the other that we'll be up in a few hours, ready to start the day all over again. Or sometimes we stop at half ten and reach for a glass of wine (maybe a tub of Booja-Booja) while we watch something on YouTube or have a little chat. On these occasions I prefer not to talk about what we're working on, as it helps me unwind before bedtime if we talk about something else. Saying that, though, I'm still able to conk out as soon as my head hits the pillow, even without a little bit of downtime.

It's a good job Tom and I are both creative and understand about that much-needed focused time of work, otherwise our marriage would be truly buggered right now. The nights we do nothing but sit together on the sofa and have a glass or two of wine are so unifying. Actually, in those moments of calm it's highly likely we're flicking through photos of the boys on our phones, reminding ourselves of how wonderful they are and, in turn, how incredibly lucky *we* are.

We're flipping knackered, obviously, but we're doing it. And that's true of all of us. I think we all like to look at others and wonder how everyone else is managing to fit everything in to their jam-packed lives, but it's something we are all doing. We're all busy and we all feel like we're constantly failing because there is so much going on. But we're doing it. We're ploughing on, and, fingers crossed, making some well-rounded, well-loved children in the process . . .

· · · · ·

There are times when external pressures stop me being able to switch off. I hate it when I'm with the boys and can feel a wave of anxiety rising and falling, like a constant reminder of the list of things I have to get done. It makes me feel as though I'm not making the most of being with them, and it's so frustrating when I'm aware of it because my time with them, whether I like to admit it or not, is limited.

Unwinding with the family is difficult when I've got a lot of work on, but Tom usually suggests putting work to one side for the night, or for the weekend, reminding me that our time together as a foursome is precious. It's something I really appreciate him doing as it puts things into perspective for me.

Actually, years ago a drama teacher of mine, who has since become a good friend (she gave me *The Secret* by Rhonda Byrne and I'll be eternally thankful to her for that), told me of an older actress she knew, who I think was in her eighties by that point. This actress had dedicated her life to the craft, spending decades giving performance after performance to a variety of theatre audiences – living the dream us actors strive for. However, one day she turned to my friend and said, 'Don't put off getting married or having children. Do it. Because when you're my age those audience members you performed for won't thank you for it and you'll just be without. They won't be there for you like a family would be.' I'm totally paraphrasing, but that was the general idea. We can pour so much time, energy, love, passion and emotion into our work, but it's up to the individual to ask themselves what they ultimately want to achieve – what the end goal might look like if they continue down that path.

My end goal is Tom and me in a house, surrounded by our huge family made up of children, grandchildren and great-grandchildren – and feeling a sense of pride and fulfilment at knowing that it all started with us.

Before we get to that point, though, I want to make sure I get a good work schedule set up once the boys start school. In an ideal world I'd love work to run in sync with term times so that Tom and I can just be with our children when they're off school. I want us to be able to go off travelling the world together, flying off on an adventure and having some proper family time . . . That's my wish. That's why I'm becoming a seasoned juggler now, while still attempting to live in the moment as much as I can. Because I know that having a dream for the future is wonderful, but it will all be redundant if I don't make the most of the amazing family I have right now.

31

PUTTING MY LIFE 'OUT THERE'

PUTTING MY LIFE 'OUT THERE'

There's no denying that I'm unconventional in the fact that I 'put myself out there'. I share details of my life on YouTube, Twitter, Instagram and Facebook – I have a weekly blog on *Hello!* online in which I share my thoughts and musings. I am very much on view.

Obviously there are limits, especially when it comes to the boys. I wouldn't say I plaster them all over social media. We're very aware of how much we post of them and try our best not to overdo it, but sometimes I simply can't help but share an adorable photo I've taken of them. I'm a proud mum, after all.

When I first started planning this book I hadn't even thought about the pictures that would be in it. So when my editor brought it up in conversation I was a little panicked. I needed time to think about what I was comfortable with – I didn't want this book to feel as if I were exploiting them in some way. I got worried. We talked and agreed that most photos of them would be like the ones I sometimes post on Instagram where their faces are largely hidden, yet still manage to capture a moment. Then I started writing, and the more I wrote the less concerned I felt; the more I realised this book is a celebration of being their mum, of them being my boys. It felt like the most natural thing to have their cherub-like faces scattered throughout the text. It would've felt empty without them.

I imagine my editor was quite shocked at the stream of family photos I eventually sent her way – full-on portraits of Buzz and Buddy, pictures that are personal and special. I wasn't tiptoeing my way around including them. They're in here and I'm immensely proud of that. After all, without them there is no mum book!

I guess I never really think of what I put out there as sharing, I just natter and post without really thinking. In fact, if people I know say they've seen or read anything I've done it catches me off guard, as though I'd rather they didn't know certain stuff about me. I sometimes forget that they might have seen what I've shared too. Perhaps communicating with strangers is the thing that I find so refreshing and appealing.

I've got so much joy and comfort from the online world. I've found mums and dads who are sympathetic and empathetic. People who just cheer me on when times get a little hairy, and remind me that everything is going to be OK. We are all different, but we're all doing what we do to get by. I like the ethos the majority of us share. Though of course there are also those who feel the need to comment in disagreement with whatever it is I've posted . . .

Last night I put up a photo of me with Buzz and Buddy on a walk – I'd had them on my own all day and wrote a short post about how lovely it had been and how the 'time out' step had only been used once. I then added that we were about to head into the witching hour, so my glee might end up being short lived. It was a nice, funny, happy little post recounting a lovely day with my boys. I was feeling great that my day with them had been largely hassle free and that we'd all enjoyed ourselves.

The comments were all largely similar, either detailing the highs and lows of their own days with their children or agreeing that the witching hours (this should be plural because it lasts way longer than an hour) are a total bitchface.

There were a few comments, though, that poked holes in my parenting. One mum listed the ages of her four children (as though displaying her credentials) before telling me that the time out step doesn't work 'long term' and that she didn't bother with it. She then wrote that cuddles and explanations are all a child needs, ending on the comment 'love not punishment, every time'.

Well, that was a fine way to hurl cowpat on my parade.

I can categorically tell you that Buzz receives plenty of love and cuddles from me, and we talk LOTS! For her to imply anything different was upsetting.

I didn't respond. There was no need. But comments in that vein linger in my mind for longer than necessary and make me doubt myself. I'm sure the lady writing them didn't mean to knock my confidence. In fact the rest of her message was complimentary, so I should've just focused on that and overlooked the other bit. I guess the hard thing is knowing that it's not just me who can read these kinds of comments – anyone and everyone can see my parenting being brought into question. That bothers me. I don't want other people looking at me and thinking I'm a bit shit . . . That sounds vainer than

I want it to, but if I were to psychoanalyse myself I'd say my feeling that way can be linked back to being bullied when I was younger, which has left me with an overwhelming need to be accepted. I choose to be honest and self-deprecating, and to point out my flaws before others can. I want to get in there first and say it before they can even think it. Having said all that, I know I'm a flipping great mum. I'm fucking great. Yes, I get it wrong sometimes, but I've learned that we all do. Never kick a mum when she's feeling good. Let her rejoice and savour that moment – because two minutes later she might be covered in poop from a toddler who refuses to defecate on the toilet while her baby pulls her thinning hair out of her sore scalp.

Just saying . . .

I feel I should point out that I don't get these sorts of comments all the time. I wouldn't consider myself someone who gets trolled or has negative abuse chucked at her that much. I don't. Not by any means. I count myself lucky in that sense, but maybe because of that I haven't formed a very thick skin. Or perhaps it's because I've allowed people to see so much of me that it feels harsh when people criticise.

Ah I'm probably overthinking it.

The other things I've posted about that have attracted people's judgment have been:

- Using a baby carrier – 'wearing' your child is a fab thing, but beware of the wave of superior knowledge from others if you're wearing the wrong sort of gear.
- Scaring Buzz on Halloween – we were throwing him a little party and I put on some face paint. I hadn't thought about how scary that might be for him when he woke up from

his nap. I posted a video of him being shocked and upset on Facebook, but left out the part where he started laughing and joining in seconds later while getting his own face painted. I should've posted the whole story like I had on YouTube; it would've prevented people being really horrible about me as a mum and my willingness to 'scar my child for life in order to get views'. I never swear online, but I seriously wanted to respond to each person who'd posted a horrible comment and tell them to fuck off . . . instead my insides curdled and I was left feeling dreadful.

- Putting my son in pink – I mean, seriously?

In moments where something I've shared has created an unwanted response I feel like I have two options: continue to trust in my own parenting techniques for my children while understanding that every child and parent are different, or stop and allow myself to get consumed by what's been said, perhaps even turning it into a mini-debate by replying. By doing the latter I'd be just like the mum I met in class when Buzz was a baby. I don't need to war with people online. I don't need to have those exchanges and get het up. Life is too short to spread anything but love and understanding – plus, I'm always more than happy to hear from other parents about how they've coped with different aspects of parenting. I love starting up those conversations. I want people to share and I welcome the chat – sometimes I even ask for advice, knowing that there will be others out there who've gone through exactly the same as I have and who can help me.

For me, social media remains a happy place for me to go and be part of a community that I love. I don't feel I need to pretend. I can just be. If I didn't have it I would probably feel lonely and isolated when going through stages of motherhood that have tested me and caught me off guard.

I don't just share the good bits (I know how much people hate seeing happy people all the time) but, as in this book, I give a more rounded version of what I'm experiencing in the hope that it'll stop others feeling alone when they aren't, and perhaps even to seek a bit of comfort when I'm in need of it.

The internet is not a bad place. It's brought us together. It's unified so many of us in a time when we're supposedly divided.

Thank you, internet.

32

THIS IS NOT A TIP BOOK,
BUT IF IT WERE . . .

THIS IS NOT A TIP BOOK, BUT IF IT WERE . . .

T his is not a tip book. I've said that many times while talking about it and indeed throughout these very pages. BUT, here are five quick things I swear by from my own experience:

- Get a headphone splitter! Amazing if you're away travelling and you both want to watch something while the baby's asleep.
- When you go out with expressed milk take a flask of boiling water with you. Then you won't need to wait for it to be brought over. I'm pretty sure there are snazzy gadgets that do this sort of thing now, but we just use a flask we already had and one of Tom's old smoothie shaker thingies to pour the water into.
- When flying, breastfeed your baby on take-off and landing to help their ears adjust to the pressure.
- Realise that YOU are your child's mum, not Janet from

down the road or the stranger who gave you a weird look when you sniffed your baby's bottom in public (it's the easiest way!). Trust your own instincts and do what you feel is right for you and your baby.

- Be honest, especially when talking to other mums. It's highly likely you'll find you're not the only one struggling in some way. Saying, 'I'm finding this hard' can be the first step to making some great mummy friends.

BONUS THOUGHT:

- Look guilt square in the eye and tell it to piss off. If you're feeling guilty then you're feeling that way because you've had to make a tough decision for the benefit of you and your family. Don't let guilt add to the weight of that. Trust you've made the right decision and get on with it.

AND ANOTHER ONE:

- Remember that no one will ever love your child as much as you do and for that reason, you are their world. If your child thinks that highly of you, then maybe you should too.

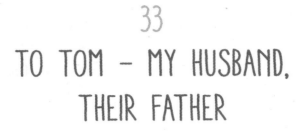

TO TOM – MY HUSBAND,
THEIR FATHER

TO TOM – MY HUSBAND, THEIR FATHER

D ude!
   I'd love to go back and tell our thirteen-year-old selves what we're doing now – that we're married and have two children and have the most hectic lives ever. I wonder what they'd make of it all. I don't think they'd believe us. The last eighteen years have been quite an adventure, but nothing compares to the last three with Buzz and Buddy (gosh, I wonder what they'd make of the names!).

Look at our boys. No seriously, look at them. We did that. Not just the actual creation of them, these living, breathing little humans, but the shaping of the people they're becoming before our eyes – they are the product of the love we've poured into them, the time we've taken to encourage and nurture them.

I love seeing you with them. You're fun, engaging and full of an energy that'll inspire them for years to come. You're more alive and passionate than I've seen you in years. I must admit that I feel boring in comparison. I'm the one with the boobs and the squidgy bits they like to cuddle – but you're the entertainer, the one they look at with a sparkle of anticipation in their eyes, knowing they're about to witness whatever magic your mind has dreamed up in that moment.

You're an amazing dad. I would say 'the best', but our dads will read this and they're pretty darn great at this parenting shizzle too.

You annoy me sometimes too, though.

No seriously, you annoy the hell out of me. But that's OK. Because I know I annoy the hell out of you, too. I get stressed out when I'm on a deadline or I have a lot of 'to do' Post-it notes stuck to my computer screen. I huff when I leave the bed at night to tend to one of the boys – sometimes with a sarcastic comment, or just a lot of heavy-footing as I sulk away from my nice warm bed. Although, to be fair, I think you actually sleep through it all anyway. That's how annoying you are.

It's not you. It's not the boys . . . Remember how much I used to sleep? I loved sleep. I miss it, you know?

But it's not you.

Sometimes I am so unreasonable – hey, maybe that's where Buzz gets it from. Let's bloody hope not. Let's just hope it's down to the terrible twos, otherwise having two of me in the house will be a nightmare for all of us.

Thank you for laughing at me when I'm ridiculous. That's what I need. Not someone who'll greet it with more crap and allow it to escalate. Just a plain laugh that tells me what a dick I'm being. That tends to snap me out of it.

I couldn't do any of this without you. I mean, I could, if I was forced to – there's always a way – but I wouldn't ever want to.

We co-parent – I think that's the term. One is no more important or needed than the other. Or perhaps I should say we co-pilot, navigating our way through uncharted territory and holding on for dear life when we get caught in the crosswinds.

Ah . . . it's flipping great though, isn't it?

I'm not sure if I'm the mum either of us thought I would be. I'm not sure if parenthood is what we thought it would be. But I can say that having a family of our own has been – HANDS DOWN – the best thing we've ever done. It's everything I could've hoped for and more. It's challenging too, obviously, but it's also come with more happy emotions than I know how to process.

I love you more since we've created life. I know we have no time to hang out any more and that date nights are few and far between, but you mean more to me now than ever before.

My life is full, because of you.

Thank you.

34

TO BUZZ AND BUDDY – MY BOYS

TO BUZZ AND BUDDY – MY BOYS

It's come to my attention that I talk a lot in this book about both of you crying. I can't lie, you did cry a lot. You still do, occasionally, although thankfully not as much as you once did. Yes, you cry. And that's fine. It's a good way of expressing your emotions, and while I hope nothing in the world makes you feel like you have to cry, I don't ever want you to feel like you can't . . .

Emotion is wonderful.

Embrace it.

Go with it.

Don't let anyone make you feel as though you can't express your thoughts and feelings. Doing so will always leave your heart feeling that little bit lighter, your soul that little bit freer.

Despite the tears, my own included, I want you to know that you make me feel more loved than I ever have before. Buzz, your kisses (especially the really, really, really long ones) are the sweetest things I've ever had the pleasure of receiving.

And Buddy, the way you squish your face into mine, as though you're trying to kiss me too, is utterly adorable – even if it does hurt me a little sometimes. I know you're just consumed with a desire to have me as close as humanly possible, and that makes me chuckle every time. That's why I never stop you.

Your smiles, the ones that are just for me, are the most magical, heartbreaking, life-affirming sights I will ever see – the glistening sparkle that appears in your eyes as your mouths widen into a happy grin.

I can't believe how lucky I am to be the one on the receiving end of such beauty.

Being a parent isn't easy, something you will learn for yourselves if you become dads in the future, but I can honestly say that being YOUR mum is the most rewarding thing I've ever done in my entire life. I gave you my body to grow in before you found your way into my arms, and you repay me yearly, monthly, weekly, daily, hourly – minute by minute, second by second.

Thank you.

This book is a collection of funny stories, a mixture of feelings evoked through an overwhelming time, and I wouldn't change any of it. A flat tummy, a full night of sleep, a day of work without feeling guilty, time to sit on a sunlounger and actually rest while feeling the sun on my skin – none of that means anything; those things carry no worth. You, my boys, are priceless. Every second we get to spend on this earth together is a blessing.

Your dad and I are so proud of every single thing that you do. We always will be.

Seek happiness.

Give love.

Follow your hearts.

ACKNOWLEDGEMENTS

Seeing as this is a non-fiction book encapsulating a chunk of my life, I feel like I have to thank every single person I've encountered over the last four years because there's every chance you've had an effect on the mother I am. Actually, I could go back way further than that and thank everyone I've ever met . . . I guess there's no chance of missing anyone out that way. Let's do that. Thanks to everyone I've met. Or not met. That's definitely everyone covered, but let's highlight a few:

Hannah Ferguson, my agent. You got me through the publishing doors in the first place; without you my writing career wouldn't exist. How lovely that we went on to become bump buddies! Big kisses to Nell!

Charlotte Hardman, my editor. Your passion and dedication to this book have been phenomenal. You absolutely 'get me', which has been so crucial when sharing something so personal. Thanks for all the late night emails and being so kind with my deadlines. I promise I'm usually early for everything else.

Ha! Big thanks to Fiona Rose for being by your side as your assistant editor.

Will Speed, thank you for your wonderful designs and cover. You've really brought this book to life.

I'd also like to thank Eleni Lawrence, Jasmine Marsh, Naomi Berwin, Joanna Kaliszewska, Catherine Worsley, Claudette Morris and everyone else at Hodder & Stoughton who've given me such a kind welcome.

Sophie Gildersleeve, Rebecca Boyce and the rest of the gang at James Grant, you rock. I feel very lucky to have such a supportive team behind me cheering me on.

My virtual friends! We're stuck in a world where the internet has gained a bit of a reputation for being full of trolls or keyboard warriors. I don't see that. I see the love. The amount of encouragement and support you give me on a daily basis is astounding. Thank you!

My family! Writing and having two children is completely different to juggling with just the one. Thank you for making such a huge effort to ensure my writing days are spent writing, and for always being there for us.

Tom, my partner in crime. You've already got a whole letter dedicated to you in here so you know exactly what I think of you. You're utterly inspiring in every way. Thanks for not getting too stressed at me when I've been stressed with dead-lines. Or, more accurately, thanks for dishing out the Booja ice-cream when needed!

My boys, Buzz and Buddy. Thank you for just being here. You light up my life in more ways than you know.

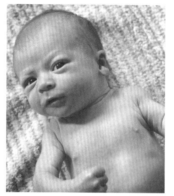
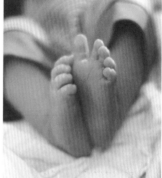